KU-524-108

B48 648 574 9

WITHDRAWN
FROM THE
ROTHERHAM
PUBLIC
LIBRARY

BERNARD INGHAM

YORKSHIRE MILLENNIUM

Yorkshire will give you peace and tranquillity in the Year of our Lord 2000 at Fountains Abbey, near Ripon, one of the magnificent relics of the early blossoming of Christianity which adorn the county.

BERNARD INGHAM

YORKSHIRE MILLENNIUM

A celebration of 1000 glorious years

First published in Great Britain 1999 by
Dalesman Publishing Company Limited
Stable Courtyard
Broughton Hall
Skipton
North Yorkshire BD23 3AZ

Text © Bernard Ingham
Photographs © Dorothy Burrows, David Coates, Richard Cochrane, Jacqui Cordingley, Chris Craggs, Alan Curtis, Deryck Hallam, Granville Harris, Roger Kilvington, Mike Kipling, John Morrison, Tom Parker, Ken Paver, Stuart Price, Colin Raw, Roger Redfern, Paul Ridsdale, Clifford Robinson, Tony Rostron, David Tarn, Simon Warner, Keith Watson

A British Library Cataloguing in Publication record is available for this book

ISBN 185568 166 8

Designed by Jonathan Newdick
Typeset by SPAN Graphics Limited
Colour Origination by Grasmere Digital Imaging Limited
Printed by Midas Printing (HK) Limited

All rights reserved. This book must not be circulated in any form of binding or cover other than that in which it is published and without similar condition of this being imposed on the subsequent purchaser. No part of this publication may be reproduced, stored on a retrieval system or transmitted in any form, or by any means, electronic, mechanical, photocopying, recording or otherwise, without either prior permission in writing from the publisher or a licence permitting restricted copying. In the United Kingdom such licences are issued by the Copyright Licensing Agency, 90 Tottenham Court Road, London, W1P 9HE. The right of Bernard Ingham to be identified as author of this work has been asserted in accordance with Copyright Designs and Patents Acts 1988.

Contents

Introduction

Lastingham Church

There is no better way to celebrate two thousand years of our Lord than through a millennium book which shares the glories of His Yorkshire with the wider world. We Yorkshiremen who live in exile feel closer to God in our native county. Those who remain loyal to it inhabit the pastures of heaven in their own minds. The "God's Own Country" of which we speak quite unselfconsciously requires no further explanation among Britons. It means Yorkshire which, incidentally, as we learned almost at birth, has more acres than words in the Bible.

For 200 years in Anglo-Saxon times, Yorkshire was the centre of the Christian faith in England. Lastingham and Whitby testify to the building then of churches and monasteries. Our very stones bear witness to centuries of worship and some provide a peace which passeth all understanding in an age from which silence has all but been banished by the internal combustion and jet engines and amplified airwaves. Is there a more restful, calming haven, a better antidote to hypertension, than the ruins of Fountains Abbey? Our hills and dales still sing His praises in churches and chapels which have survived our great post-war secularisation and multiculturalism. Not everybody yet worships on Sunday morning at the supermarket or peering into a car boot.

Other buildings such as the hexagonal 18th century church in Heptonstall, just above my native Hebden Bridge, are monuments to a Methodism which is widely credited with inoculating the aspiring industrial masses of the West Riding against Marxism. Ampleforth Abbey developed in Cardinal Basil Hume a leader of English Roman Catholics of great piety and immense political skill for nearly a quarter of a century. And for as long as Christians can remember, York, with a Yorkshire-born Archbishop in David Hope now in Bishopthorpe Palace, has been the second ecclesiastical city after Canterbury, not to mention occasionally the seat of temporal national government.

Yorkshire can bring from its infinite variety of countryside – dale, moor, vale, plain, bog, coast, estuary, lake and hill – a tremendous

pageant of Christian witness to the millennium. Yet, officially, it came fairly late to Christianity – 627 years late to be precise. I suppose we have three people to thank for eventually making it: St Aidan, of Lindisfarne, for his missionary work among the heathens of Deira, the Anglo-Saxon equivalent of Yorkshire; Ethelburga, Christian daughter of the rulers of Kent and wife of the unbelieving but tolerant Edwin, son of the King of Deira; and Paulinus, a Christian priest who came with the Pope's commendation to live in Edwin's court. Between them, wife and priest eventually prevailed upon Edwin to be baptised in celebration of his vanquishing the West Saxons to become to all intents and purposes the boss of England outside Kent.

He took the faith on Easter Day 627 in the forerunner of York Minster, a little chapel he knocked up for his conversion along with many of his Witan – council of elders – and even his high priest. This chap, by the name of Coifi, was obviously a Yorkshireman: he did not do things by halves. He took the view that, having been baptised, he had better get rid of the trappings of his old religion. So off he went to his heathen temple near Market Weighton and not only threw his lance at it but urged the populace to join him in destroying it. Yorkshire's first anti-heathen riot promptly ensued. We have not looked back since, give or take a setback or two such as the unholy elimination of a thousand years of history by Edward Heath in 1974 when, at a stroke, as it were, he did for Yorkshire and its administrative ridings (thirds) with his local government re-organisation.

Technically, we are no more, as dead, deceased and kaput as John Cleese's parrot. We "passed out of existence", as the Encyclopaedia Britannica bleakly puts it, to become "a former county". When I was Margaret Thatcher's press secretary, Sir Edward, as he now is, once called me "a menace to the constitution". He obviously knows what he is talking about.

It is not, however, in the nature of Yorkshiremen to be prevented from singing their county's praises just because some misguided politician has done away with it in a mad moment of legislative excess. I certainly do not propose to be put off. Yorkshire to me is not just some tract of land enclosed by a boundary drawn on a map at the whim of the Prime Minister, or a mere name deriving from our Viking ancestry, as

Below and left. York Minster and its restored rose window

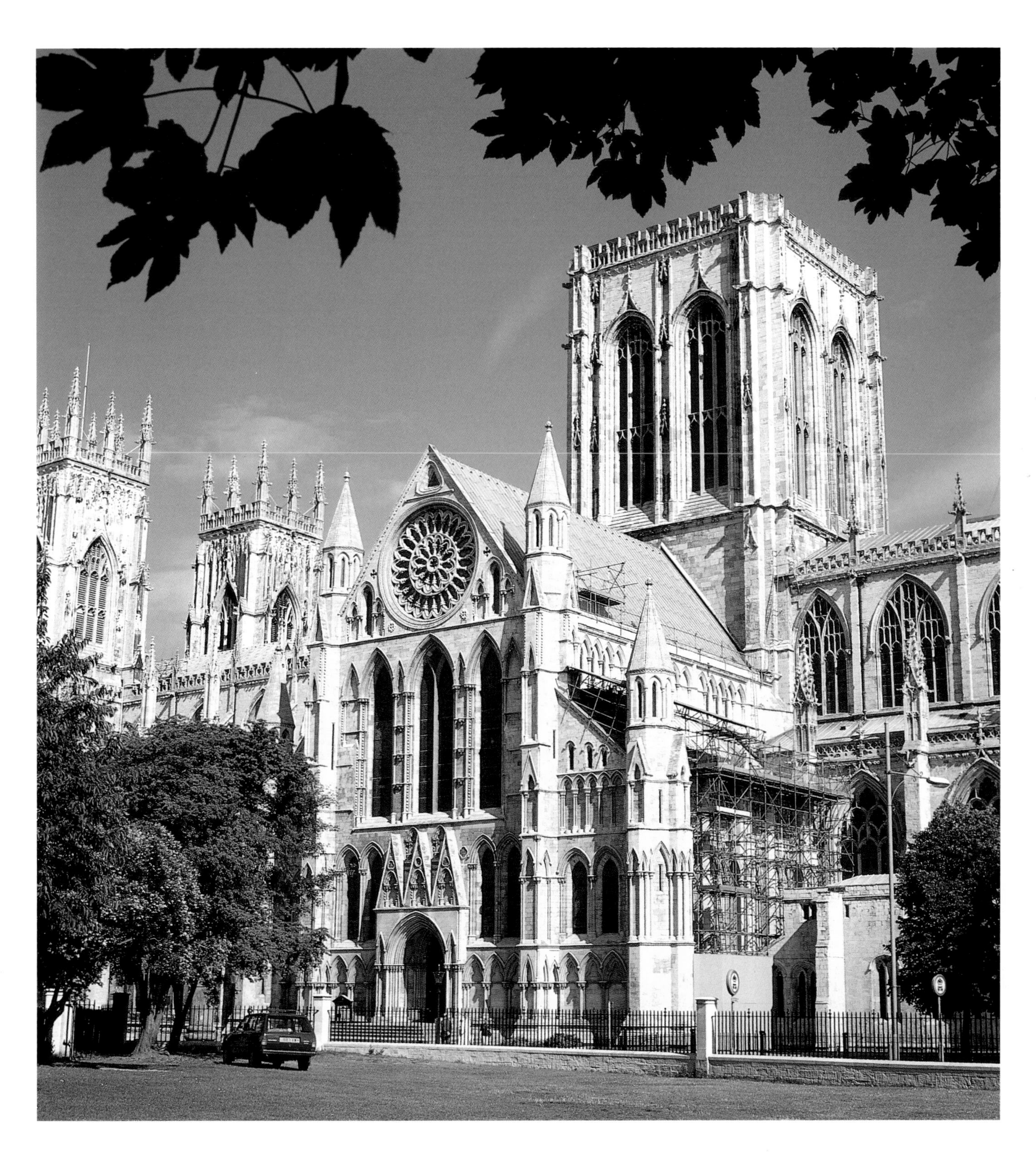

evidenced by York's pungently realistic Jorvik museum.

It inspires a mystical sense of belonging and confers a state of grace – or used to do before Yorkshire County Cricket Club, for commercial reasons, sacrilegiously dispensed with the need to make sure that your wife gave birth well within its borders so that your son could, without doubt, be qualified to play for it. Freddie Trueman and I, among many others, have not felt the same since. Yet, however much we may despair of the corruptions of the modern world being visited upon our heritage, we remain convinced that as Yorkshiremen we are something special and many would say unique, not least in the eyes of our Saviour.

But what constitutes that speciality, that uniqueness? How does it bind together a people who offer the six distinctive delights which the Yorkshire Tourist Board might use as a marketing ploy – the South Riding, Pennines, Dales, Vale of York, North York Moors and Yorkshire Coastal experiences? What, if anything, have the industrial masses of the south west in common with the county types of North Yorkshire other than their annual meeting at the Great Yorkshire Show at Harrogate? And where, if that uniqueness exists, whether tangibly or spiritually, does it come from?

Let's start with our geography. We are, it is said, all products of our environment. But our environment is anything but homogenous. In the west and north we are hill dwellers; in the centre and east plainsmen and seafarers, though with a Wolds bump in the middle which, when our winters brought snow, took Yorkshire Post reporters ritually to the relief of Wetwang and Fridaythorpe. The Industrial Revolution divided us further – the south western third blighted by Blake's "dark, satanic mills" and the north-western two thirds a rural idyll, fringed by steam, smoke and murk along the Tees and Humber estuaries. You can't typify a Yorkshireman.

Our history isn't much help, either, in providing the key to our binding sense of belonging to a superior tribe. I have found it singularly profitless delving into prehistoric Yorkshire, littered though the county is with the remains of the Stone, Bronze and Iron Ages from the limestone caves above Settle to the Neolithic barrows, or burial mounds, of the Wolds and the Celtic Iron-Age settlement at Stanwick, near Richmond. You had to be tenacious and resourceful to survive anywhere in

England in those days.

The Romans gave us our basic road system between a host of military stations such as Eboracum (York), Olicana (Ilkley), Cataractonium (Catterick) and Danum (Doncaster). Roads help in the binding process. But the Romans came and went within 400 years without leaving much trace of their hot, Latin blood unless it has belatedly come out in our undoubted capacity for tunnel-visioned passion about cricket both on the field and in the factionalism off it which has blighted most of Yorkshire CCC's last unrewarding 30 years.

I like to think that Yorkshiremen (and the cartoonists' fierce Yorkshirewomen who keep their men in order, like some early Margaret Thatcher, with a rolling pin) got seriously down to character building in the latter part of the Dark Ages of Anglo-Saxon England. That at least is the theory of our late Poet Laureate, Ted Hughes, who was born in Mytholmroyd, a wonderfully romantic Old English way of describing the clearing at the confluence of the Calder and Elphin streams in my native Upper Calder Valley. We can trace our ancestry, he reckons, to the matings of Celts, who made their last independent stand there in the western rampart of Elmet, with the Vikings, who brought their adventurous animal spirits and place names up the Humber, and the rogues and vagabonds who sought refuge in the moorland fastnesses that later inspired the Brontë sisters to their several masterpieces.

There are many who say that no one should waste another moment seeking the clue to my turbulent nature. That may be so, but "a cross between Heathcliff and a pit bull terrier", as the late Jean Rook, Yorkshire's self-styled First Lady of Fleet Street, described me, is not necessarily a reliable guide to the origins of the overall Yorkshire being. In fact, I think it merely explains the Pennine contribution to that total character – a strain which puts awkwardness into Lancashire folk as well as Yorkshire people. That rugged, millstone, gritty independence is revealed – or at least was until, as I see it, the aberration of Tony Blair's landslide general election victory in 1997 – in the astonishing number of marginal Parliamentary seats in industrial West Yorkshire and East Lancashire.

They don't come much more angular, taciturn, private, single-minded, stubborn, opinionated, gallows-humoured, determined or industrious

Brontë Parsonage, Haworth

than true Pennine people. They provide the caricature for Yorkshiremen as a whole. Somehow, you know that it was a Pennine town, not Harrogate or York, where Ashley Jackson, the Holmfirth artist, having been asked to switch on the Christmas lights for "nowt", was pressed by the organiser "to bring along someone famous an' all". But you can't be sure, can you, because tact is not a Yorkshireman's strong suit.

I prefer to call it honesty – the sort of honesty which the Normans encountered in all Anglo-Saxons but especially, I am convinced, in the Yorkshire variety. It is described by Rudyard Kipling in his poem in which a dying Norman baron advises his son how to treat the Saxons:

"The Saxon is not like us Normans. His manners are not so polite.
But he never means anything serious till he talks about justice and
right.
When he stands like an ox in the furrow with his sullen set eyes on your
own,
And grumbles, 'This isn't fair dealing,' my son, leave the Saxon alone."

It is a pity that the son did not heed that advice. Yorkshire's Saxons found their Norman French overlords, with their alien ways, oppressive and irksome. They rebelled and, far from leaving them alone, the Normans exacted terrible revenge which is chronicled by the word "waste" that appears so monotonously in the Domesday Book. It signifies the result of William the Conqueror's "Harrying of the North" which left Yorkshire a blasted heath, fit only for hunting by the King and his 29 "tenants in chief" when they ventured out of their castles.

I fear these cruel Normans reinforced the best and worst tendencies in Yorkshiremen – their grim determination and their protective isolationism, their utter conviction that the grass is far from greener on the other side of the fence, as Lesley Garrett's father warned her when she went to seek fame and fortune as an opera singer in London. "What do yer want to go to London for?" he demanded. "It's nowt but 20 Doncasters end to end". Precisely.

After these formative years for the Yorkshire character, the county became the battle ground of the Middle Ages. The Scots fought over it with, as well as without, the support of independent-minded Yorkshire barons who gave King John no end of trouble. Those barons were not

Hebden Bridge

noted for their constancy or for their unwavering support for the White Rose of Yorkshire during the Wars of the Roses. Ironically, this 30-year turmoil did anything but bind Yorkshire together. On the one hand, the Percys with estates in all three ridings, the Cliffords of Skipton and the Talbots of Hallamshire were Lancastrians whereas the Nevilles, Scropes and Latimers of the North Riding were Yorkists. At times, it seemed less like a Yorkshire/Lancashire conflict than a Yorkshire civil war within a North/South argument and with Yorkshire even a Lancastrian stronghold.

It is all very confusing for those of us searching for clues to the making of Yorkshire clannishness as distinct from the Yorkshire character. It is even more frustrating to discover that the Wars of the Roses mostly passed the ordinary folk by, except, for example, when they had to clean up after the gentry had left Cock Beck flowing with Yorkist and Lancastrian blood after the awesome battle of Towton. Not much evidence here that the episode you would have thought would have had a defining influence on the Yorkshire identity had much, if anything, to do with it at all. Worse still, the whole blessed episode was settled the wrong way at Bosworth in 1485 with "that noble son of York", Richard III, offering his kingdom for a horse before he lost it and his life and the Yorkist cause. Not even Yorkshiremen, in all their perversity, could surely found their legend on an ignominious defeat.

But it gets worse. In the Civil War it was estimated that 242 Yorkshire families supported the King, 128 were Parliamentarians, 69 were either divided or prone to change sides while 240 remained true to type, deciding to "see all, hear all and say nowt". This contrary lot inevitably spilt Yorkshire blood all over the county while Cromwell knocked the British Isles about a bit. You may well therefore reasonably conclude that there seems to be more in their geography and history that divides Yorkshiremen than unites them. And there will be many who say Amen to that after the recent bitter turmoil in Yorkshire CCC between the Geoffrey Boycott pros and antis. Mr Boycott may have been – nay, still is – the Greatest Living Englishman in the eyes of some. But he still causes division, which seems to be par for the course for Yorkshiremen.

Seven years ago Sir Ranulph Twistleton-Wykeham-Fiennes, to give the distinguished explorer his Sunday name, actually announced to the world that never again would he take a Yorkshireman on one of his expeditions. "You can say that is generalising," he said. "Once bitten twice shy and several times bitten, then you make a rule about it. People from Yorkshire, we have found, are dour and nurse a grudge. One thing you can't put up with on expeditions are people who search for trouble, then nurse it when they have found it."

So where does all this sense of Yorkshire pride come from, given that we are such awkward cusses – and not just towards treble-barrelled explorers but also with our own kind? Is it the belated product of the Industrial Revolution, perhaps nothing more than a form of sporting opium, based on cricket, for the labouring masses? Or does it lie in the genes of the people of whom Pennine mongrels like me are outlandish examples? Or is it a combination of the two? And, if so, why is it that the men of the North and East Ridings are no less proud of their identity? Why, indeed, is the urge to identify so great that 90 per cent of *Dalesman's* circulation is outside the Yorkshire Dales?

To come up with some sort of answer, I think we have first to recognise that Yorkshire has been maturing as a concept for a thousand years, bolstered by the position for so long of York, the county capital, as effectively England's second city. Ted Heath's meddling with our boundaries and ridings a mere quarter of a century ago has done nothing to interfere with that process. If anything, he has reinforced it. We don't take kindly to offcumdens mucking us about. The old Norman baron discovered that among our ancestors circa 1066.

The continuing desire to recover all the ridings within our ancient boundaries underlines the point. And where else would you expect the English backlash against all this Celtic devolution nonsense to start but in Yorkshire? The clamour for a Yorkshire Parliament may owe more to the jobs-for-the-boys-and-girls syndrome – or to a political need to stir some interest in regionalism among the apathetic English – than the idea itself. But Yorkshire was the obvious and perhaps the only place where a backlash might reasonably convincingly occur outside Cornwall. The fact that all sorts of Yorkshireman have laughed the idea of a Yorkshire Parliament off Flamborough Head into the depths of the North Sea only goes to show that the contrary gene in their DNA is fully functional alongside their desire to exert their identity.

Yet it surely stands to reason that, whereas the Romans established the fundamentals of our road system and the Normans chronicled our basic pattern of settlements, it was not until the Industrial Revolution opened up communications eight centuries later with turnpikes, canals and railways that Yorkshire's sense of belonging really became a coherent phenomenon. It was supercharged by the development of local and regional newspapers and, of course, The Yorkshire Post on which I worked in Halifax and Leeds for nine years. Yorkshire Television may not be owned by Yorkshire Television any more than The Yorkshire Post is by the Yorkshire Conservative Newspaper Company. Indeed, Yorkshire Television has fallen into the hands of the Lancastrian Granada. But nobody thinks of ridding themselves of Yorkshire in their title. They daren't. In any case, Yorkshire has become a powerful brand name, even if only vestiges of the Yorkshire created by the Industrial Revolution – coal, steel, wool, worsted, cotton, ready-made clothing and trawling – remain to employ its peculiar inhabitants.

No doubt the passion for the Yorkshire dialect almanac from the mid-19th century helped to stimulate a Yorkshire pride and create the legend. At one stage, the English Dialect Society counted 36 published in the West Riding alone. My grandfather gave me copies of one of the most famous, Hartley's Halifax Illuminated Clock Almanack, a mixture of mirth and morality. It sold 80,000 copies in its heyday.

We are indebted to a later student of the dialect, Dr Arnold Kellett, editor of the Yorkshire Dialect Society's Transactions, for a recent history of the county anthem, "On Ilkla Moor Baht 'At". It is a bit of a let down to discover that the hymn tune, "Cranbrook", to which it is sung, comes from Kent, like the Queen who 1,273 years ago helped to convert us to Christianity. The meaning of the song is clear for those of us who understand the native tongue. It's all about a lad on a choir trip to Ilkley Moor being teased about the potentially fatal consequences of catching a cold by sloping off "a coortin Mary Jane" without wearing a hat rather than, curiously, from lying in the damp grass or more likely heather. But who on earth composed the words and first sang them is a matter for endless speculation, apart from a choirmaster and his choristers from some West Riding chapel.

The verses bring out the Yorkshireman's morbid sense of humour and

Sir Titus Salt, Bradford

his preoccupation with death. The chorister's remains are progressively devoured by worms and then vicariously by ducks and, by feasting on a dinner of duck à l'orange, by his fellow members of the choir who, having "etten" him, get their own back on him. It is not the most inspiring lyric for England's premier county. But then Yorkshiremen (and women) would not be unique if not singular.

Wherever you mine our history you come up with the awkward squad. Take, for example, John Wycliffe, from Hipswell, near Richmond, who translated the Bible into English and advocated radical egalitarian ideas. His followers, the Lollards, were deep into the Peasants' Revolt. Robert Aske, from the Derwent Valley, led the "Pilgrimage of Grace" against Henry VIII's Dissolution of the Monasteries and, like Wycliffe, paid for it with a painful death. At least 10 of the conspirators in the Catholic Gunpowder Plot to blow up Parliament, which is celebrated every November 5 throughout the land, were from Yorkshire. The effigy of one of them, Guy Fawkes, from St Peter's School, York, sits atop every commemorative bonfire, except at his old school. That's fame through awkwardness for you – and fierce Yorkshire loyalty, too.

Then there is William Wilberforce, the politician and philanthropist from Hull who abolished the slave trade and then slavery in the British Dominions; Richard Oastler, of Bradford, who attacked child labour as "Slavery in Yorkshire"; Sir Titus Salt, who created a model village for his workers at Saltaire; and Joseph Rowntree, of York, who built an adult education movement on top of mechanics' institutes, first established by Dr John Birkbeck, of Settle. None of these were comfortable people in their time. Nor were the Luddites, the machine breakers fighting for their crafts against mechanisation, or the Chartists, struggling for Parliamentary representation for the working class, who had such strong roots in Yorkshire.

The Brontës, J. B. Priestley, Henry Moore, David Hockney, Ted Hughes, the late Prime Minister, Harold Wilson and archetypically the horseman, Harvey Smith – not to mention Herbert Sutcliffe, Len Hutton, Freddie Trueman and Geoffrey Boycott – brought or still bring a striking and arresting individuality to their work and their county. But can there be a greater – or more awkward – Yorkshireman than Captain Cook, from Marton-in-Cleveland? As the Encyclopaedia

Britannica puts it, he "set new standards of thoroughness in discovery and seamanship, in navigation, cartography, and the sea care of men, in relations with natives both hostile and docile, in the application of science at sea" and in "peacefully changing the map of the world more than any other single man in history". Only an awkward man could in the 18th century have made the health of his sailors a byword.

Don Mosey, the cricket commentator and Dalesman, was once provoked to describe Yorkshiremen as "rude, boorish, stubborn, aggressive, argumentative, intolerant and just plain downright bloody-minded". Independent testimony comes from the Oxford English Dictionary which attributes "boorishness, cunning, sharpness or trickery" to us Tykes. And "tyke" is defined not only as a Yorkshireman but as "a cur, low fellow".

By now you will have got the picture. A Yorkshireman is not a pretty sight. He has in him a sense of almost racial belonging which has developed over at least 1,000 years across his broad acres. Yorkshire acres are not, of course, just ordinary ones. It is a pride which accommodates much dissent and rebellion. The tradition of stubbornly "going your own road" is almost consciously cultivated in the hills but has flowed down the rivers to infect the whole of the Yorkshire body politic. And this Yorkshire persona, marinated across the centuries, has developed a certain piquancy since the Industrial Revolution provided the means for its cultivation and communication. The millennium finds us revelling in it. "Lord bless us sinners as we eat our dinners" is our standard grace.

I have a word of advice for foreigners – ie non-Yorkshire folk – who have to deal with us: do not take us at our own valuation. While we are very happy, for example, to be described as thick as two planks and Scots shorn of all charity, we have taken jolly good care also to acquire a reputation for incredible shrewdness and the last word in hospitality. The truth is that we are a complex lot who are only explicable in our wilfulness. God will, of course, forgive us this millennium. After all, He's One of Us.

A Place in History

The two storey, nine-bay central block of the palace – for that is the only way to describe it – of Castle Howard is flanked by single storey wings. Sadly, fire destroyed the dome and gutted most of the south side in 1940 when occupied by an evacuated girls' school.

The exquisite grounds are within a sham rampart with eleven towers. Among the lawns, scenic lakes, rose gardens and woodlands are a mausoleum and a fountain with Atlas holding a globe decorated with signs of the zodiac. The globe was brought by the Howard family from the Paris Exhibition in 1889.

Inside there is a stunning collection of paintings, sculpture, furniture, porcelain, plasterwork and Vanbrugh's grand staircase and even grander great hall. The whole effect is rather theatrical. It certainly shows you what can happen when you give an unlikely genius his head – and your brass!

Mighty castles and gracious houses illustrate the civilising of Yorkshire across the millennia – or at least the second millennium, the passing of which we're marking with this book. Castles of increasing sophistication offered protection against marauders from Scotland and over the North Sea and from ambitious English, not to say Yorkshire, lords and barons who sought advancement by the sword.

In the end – which can be pretty accurately fixed as 1649 with the conclusion of the Civil War – Yorkshire's castles were strong and defiant and a confounded nuisance to Oliver Cromwell. They withstood sieges for months and Cromwell ordered eight of Yorkshire's proudest to be rendered useless in war: Knaresborough, Cawood, Middleham, Bolton, Crayke, Helmsley, Wressle and Skipton.

In 50 years or so the gentry had forgotten about castles, except to renovate them as country seats as, for example, at Skipton which the remarkable Lady Anne Clifford, of the Royalist family, made fit for a lord again. Within our rudimentary parliamentary democracy and behind our moat formed by the North Sea, Yorkshire looked forward with new confidence. From 1700 England's largest county embarked across the ridings on a creative orgy, bringing distinguished architecture and sculptured landscapes to elegant, warm, stone country houses with treasures rich beyond the dreams of avarice of the humble herdsman employed on the great estates.

Some of the marvellous results of man's genius – of Vanbrugh, Robert Adam, Chippendale and Capability Brown – are shown in these pages. It took hundreds of years to get this far from the mound and wooden defences of the early Clifford's Tower in York. The fortified glories of Middleham, Scarborough, Richmond – probably the oldest stone-built castle in England – and beautiful Conisbrough followed. Bolton Castle shows you they were getting there because this 14th century redoubt was more comfortable and elegant than earlier ones. Perhaps that is why Mary Queen of Scots was imprisoned there. But get there Yorkshire did. And in the deer park at Studley Royal, with its vista of Ripon Cathedral, you know it did indeed come to find gracious, civilised living.

Newby Hall, a late 17th century treasure, was built by the local MP, Sir Edward Blackett. Fifty years later it was bought by the Weddell family who added wings. Its east front was designed by John Carr to accommodate the proceeds of a Grand Tour – notably a collection of Roman sculpture and a set of Gobelin tapestries. Robert Adam designed the sumptuous interior. He really excelled himself in the tapestry room. This is Yorkshire country living in all its sophistication.

The Italianate mansion of Brodsworth Hall is set on a rural island in former coal mining country. It was built from the proceeds of an interminable will dispute which formed the model for Jarndyce v Jarndyce in *Bleak House*, Charles Dickens' skit on the madly slow grind of the wheels of justice. Indeed the case went on so long – 60 years – that Brodsworth Hall was built on the interest that accrued. The £700,000 capital awarded by the House of Lords remained intact. Charles Sabine Thellusson used his money to splendid advantage: it is one of Britain's greatest Victorian country houses and was opened to the public in 1995.

Duncombe Park, the stately home of Lord and Lady Feversham, was originally built to a design first published by Sir John Vanbrugh who was responsible for Castle Howard. But the present interiors mostly date from 1895 when the house was rebuilt after a major fire six years earlier. They are a fine example of a grand interior with English and Continental furniture and splendid family portraits.

The Victorian gardens overlook Ryedale and Helmsley Castle and the trees of Duncombe Park are magnificent.

The National Trust have combined with the National Portrait Gallery to make Beningbrough Hall, north-west of York, an important gallery as well as an exquisite Georgian Hall completed in 1716 for John Bourchier.

Conisbrough's 12th century castle was the home of Hamelin Plantagenet, 5th Earl of Warren, who rode 50 miles north by west to hunt in the hills where the author was brought up. It is one of the oldest Norman cylindrical keeps in Britain and a reminder in the industrial south of Yorkshire of the former Norman presence. Sir Walter Scott chose it as the setting for his novel *Ivanhoe* while staying in the district in 1811.

Sledmere House, between Driffield and Malton, is the home of the Sykes family, the Leeds merchants renowned for 150 years of folly building. The present house was begun by Richard Sykes in 1751. Sir Christopher Sykes, an agricultural reformer, had Capability Brown landscape a park and added large wings in the 1780s. It was rebuilt after a fire in 1911 as a Georgian mansion with marvellous Edwardian workmanship.

Pages 24-27. No wonder they chose Castle Howard as the TV/film set for *Brideshead Revisited*. It is a romantic place with a romantic story.

Charles Howard, 3rd Earl of Carlisle, a Whig courtier and 2nd Lord of the Treasury, decided to rebuild Henderskelfe Castle. He didn't get very far with the Comptroller of His Majesty's Works. So he appointed an unlikely architect – John Vanbrugh, a soldier having a run of success as a playwright, with only theatrical design experience.

Perhaps Vanbrugh's best qualification was his membership, with the Earl of Carlisle, of the exclusive Kit Kat Club. Castle Howard is certainly testimony to the wisdom of appointing someone whose company you enjoy, provided, perhaps, they are supported by a self-effacing expert, a certain Nicholas Hawksmoor.

Vanbrugh's first architectural composition is a beautiful, spectacular, 18th century, baroque country estate.

Castle Howard is one of those places which keep Kodak stockholders happy. There is something stunning at every turning. A symphony in stone, lawns, lakes, water gardens and treasures. It also includes a temple (below), Vanbrugh's Temple of the Four Winds. It was his last work, executed from 1724–6. The central cube is surmounted by a dome and sits on a podium extending out as entrance steps. You can see Francesco Vassalli's interior plasterwork through glazed doors.

Four miles south of Wetherby is the earliest of the great landscape gardens of Yorkshire. The magnesian-limestone house of Bramham Park was finished by 1710, according to an authorititive book of architectural design published in 1717. The architect is not known but it seems that the designer was the owner, Robert Benson, later Lord Bingley, a self-made man and Lord Mayor and MP for York. He was a favourite of Queen Anne whose portrait, by Kneller, hangs above the fireplace in the entrance hall.

Benson was clearly a man of many parts. Having designed the house, he then set about the grounds. To the west, he laid out formal gardens in the French style. These are remarkably intact. Magnificent beech trees form avenues giving vistas of temples, statues, an obelisk, water features and the house. The pleasure grounds are separated by a retaining wall from the surrounding park. A sloping lawn falls away to a series of fountains and ponds in stepped levels. To the south is a dramatic stable block. Mr Benson deserved his peerage for bringing elegance and distinction to a bit of rural Yorkshire.

It is not the sort of place you expect to find within four miles of the centre of a great industrial and commercial city.

Nor would you imagine it had anything to do with the Knights Templars, the religious military order formed to protect pilgrims to the Holy Land. But Temple Newsam's site in Leeds once belonged to the Knights Templars – hence its name. The courtyard plan house was also the birthplace in 1545 of Henry, Lord Darnley, second husband of Mary Queen of Scots.

It was largely demolished in the 17th century, apart from one range. The U-plan house then created is now a Leeds City Museum and Art Gallery with spectacular collections of furniture, paintings, silver and porcelain. Capability Brown was also here, landscaping the park.

It is entirely appropriate that the English Civil War and Sealed Knot Societies should take Yorkshire folk back to the Great Rebellion of 1642–49, as the English Civil War is called. At least fourteen of its battles were fought on Yorkshire soil, including Marston Moor on the Plain of York where 45,000 men – 29,000 foot soldiers and 16,000 cavalry – battled it out over seven hours. Oliver Cromwell was slightly wounded but came out the winner. Two re-enactments of those battles – Alcomden Moor (top) and Adwalton Moor (bottom) – are depicted here, "fought" by the Sealed Knot Society. The English Civil War Society commemorates the three-month siege of Helmsley Castle (centre) which was one of the eight Yorkshire castles Cromwell later ordered to be rendered unfit for use in war.

The English Civil War stemmed from King Charles I's expensive scrap with Scotland. After governing without Parliament for eleven years, he was forced to summon it to get the necessary cash. Parliament refused. The signal for the start of the hostilities between the Roundheads (Parliamentarians) and Cavaliers (Royalists) was the King's rejection in York, which he was visiting on his way south from Scotland, of the Parliamentarians' Nineteen Propositions. After a year's desultory fighting, the Queen's presence in York inspired the Royalists to victory at Adwalton Moor, near Morley, winning effective control of Yorkshire. A year later in the yo-yo war Cromwell whipped the King's Men at Marston Moor, but not before they had drawn his blood. Eventually Parliament prevailed, the Commonwealth and Protectorate were established and the English Nonconformist tradition, so strong in West Yorkshire, was fostered.

The approach to Markenfield Hall, just south of Ripon, up a farm track called Hellwath is not what you would expect to a splendid, decorated, period moated manor house dating from the 14th century. It is very well connected. Exchequer Chancellor John de Markenfield was given a licence to crenellate it in 1310. Queen Elizabeth confiscated it after the Rising of the North and granted it to her Lord Keeper, Sir Thomas Egerton. Then Mr Speaker Fletcher Norton, later Baron Grantley, bought it in 1782. The 7th Lord Grantley shares the buildings with his farming tenants.

Below. All eighteen feet of the tiny chapel of St Mary, Lead sit alone in a field near Saxton. It reputedly sheltered the wounded from England's bloodiest battle – Towton (1461).

Visitors to Walmgate Bar in York should thank protest groups for what they find. In the early 19th century, the city fathers wanted to pull down the bar walls. There was pressure to remove the ancient gateways which were designed to keep the invaders out but not for the convenience of traders coming in. The town council was also short of cash to restore a bridge and saw its salvation in selling the bars' stone. Conservationists were outraged by this philistinism and saved the gateways but not all the barbicans. Walmgate is the sole exception. It is the most complete of all the city's bars. Its portcullis hangs in its slot and its 15th century wooden door still has its wicket gate.

By the 13th century, prosperous Beverley had a defensive ditch with four gates or bars. The North Bar is the only survivor and was built in 1409-10 in small, handmade bricks of irregular size and dark brown in colour. The gates remain inside the outer arch and there is a portcullis slot within the inner arch.

In Roman times, Bootham Bar was the Prima Porta Dextra, the western entrance to York into High Petergate, the old Roman Via Principa to the city centre. Today High Petergate opens out into a magnificent view of the western front of York Minster.

The fortified manor house of Ripley Castle north of Harrogate has been the home of the Ingilbys for nearly 700 years. The estate is a tremendous advertisement for hereditary responsibility in an age which has it in for hereditary peers. It is the home of excellent individual quality shops in a village remodelled in the 1820s on a settlement in Alsace-Lorraine. Set in a deer park, with a lake, it is a fascinating place, from its Civil War memorabilia to its national hyacinth collection and rare vegetables. And, yes, Capability Brown was here, too.

There is something rather sweet – as well as immensely grand – about Harewood House between Leeds and Harrogate. It was built in honey-coloured sandstone with West Indian sugar money by Edwin Lascelles, a Whig MP, in 1759.

And it is magnificent.

Lascelles brought together a formidable team – John Carr, architect; Robert Adam, interior designer, as he would now be described; and, of course, Capability Brown. They have left their mark all over Yorkshire. Only the best craftsmen and materials were used. And, Sir Charles Barry added Italianate flourishes in 1843.

Capability Brown got through £6,000 in those days in landscaping the park – a lake, belts of trees, vistas to Almscliff Crag away to the north west, not to mention the ruined Harewood Castle to play with.

William Lord Aldburgh crenellated the castle in 1367. His daughters married into families who held it until the late 16th century. Then came the Lascelles who own it to this day.

Harewood House is now the home of the Earl and Countess of Harewood and a focus for tourists, conferences and students of architecture, Chippendale furniture, contemporary art, English watercolours and ornithology. It has an internationally renowned bird garden.

One of the bonuses of working for the *Yorkshire Post* was, the author decided, playing cricket in the grounds of Harewood. It was even a pleasure to come away with a duck on a beautiful June day. Yorkshire living at its most glorious.

Left. The last Yorkshire castle to fall to the Parliamentary forces during the Civil War was Skipton, fortress of the Cliffords, the King's men. It surrendered in December 1645 and subsequently was one of the eight Yorkshire castles required by Parliament to be rendered unfit for use in war. The part open to the public dates from 1200 and the round towers from the 14th century when the Cliffords became Lords of Skipton. George Clifford, 3rd Earl of Cumberland, was Queen Elizabeth's Champion. His daughter, Lady Anne, restored the castle after its Civil War siege and the early Tudor entrance has an inscription commemorating her work.

Right and below. Guarding the entrance to Swaledale is Richmond Castle, another fine Norman stronghold built to subdue rebellious Yorkshiremen. Its hundred feet high keep with walls eleven feet thick was added to the gatehouse a hundred years later by Henry II. He needn't have been so defensive: one reason the castle is in such a remarkable condition is that it was never besieged.

The medieval town of Richmond grew beside the castle. It was walled in 1311 against marauding Scots.

The Franciscans, who date back to 1258 in Richmond, gave the town its most attractive medieval building – the slender Grey Friar's Tower.

Trinity Chapel, in the market place, has become the regimental museum of the Green Howards, one of Yorkshire's famous regiments.

Wheeldale Roman Road was built to connect the Roman fort at Malton with the coast, somewhere near Whitby, and could have been a trade route for jet which the Romans prized for jewellery and ornaments. The mile-long stretch of cambered and culverted road across heather-covered moorland has remarkably survived 2000 years.

Practical Pickering has park benches in the ruins of its 11th century motte and bailey castle – a defence consisting of an earthen mound (motte) topped by a wooden tower within a bailey, an enclosure defended by a ditch and palisades. And why not? It's wonderful we find peace amid ruins from a fierce period in these parts.

In what is now racehorse country lie the magnificent ruins of Middleham Castle. It was the second fort to be built here. A motte and bailey castle was erected by Ribald of Brittany in 1086 on William's Hill to guard Coverdale. A century later his grandson, Robert FitzRanulph, built a stone castle a quarter of a mile away which eventually came by marriage to that noble son of York, Richard III. And so Middleham became known as the "Windsor of the North". Richard reinforced it with turrets and towers but sadly it declined with his death on Bosworth field.

Pontefract is described as one of the least known of England's great historical towns – surprising as Richard II died in its castle and Shakespeare gave it notoriety as "Bloody Pomfret" in his play of the deposed king. The castle was a major Royalist stronghold in the Civil War and destroyed soon after although its ruins can still be seen (below).

It looks wonderful on a spring day, set solidly on a mound of dancing daffodils. But Clifford's Tower is also a monument to ethnic cleansing. It goes back to Norman times. When Aldred, Archbishop of York, crowned William the Conqueror in Westminster Abbey, some Yorkshire earls paid homage to him. But a couple of them, Edwin and Morcar, soon rose against him, bringing William to York to put down rebellion. On the second occasion, in 1068, he sacked the city and killed hundreds of its inhabitants before erecting a wooden fort for the garrison he left behind to replace the one burned down in the revolt. That fort almost certainly stood on the mound where Clifford's Tower, probably named after the powerful Yorkshire family, now sits. The stone building was completed in 1270.

During the 12th century, York became an important commercial and administrative centre, attracting hundreds of Jews who lived there under the King's protection. They prospered as money lenders – usury was forbidden to Christians – and as merchants. But their Christian neighbours feared and hated them and things began to come to a head at the London coronation of Richard I in 1189.

Superstition had it that a Jewish presence at the celebrations would be a bad omen for the reign. Two Jews from York, bearing gifts for the King, were set upon. When the widow and family of one were killed in York in March 1190 the city's Jewish population took refuge in Clifford's Tower. Threatened with death, many Jews killed themselves, fathers slaughtering their families. Those who were left were murdered when the mob broke in. The Jewish quarter was put to the torch. There is a plaque to their memory at the foot of the mound.

Below. The summer palace of Philippa, Edward III's queen, Knaresborough Castle is now a municipal park towering above the Nidd Gorge. It was appropriately a Royalist stronghold in the Civil War but the Parliamentarians rendered it uninhabitable after the siege following the Battle of Marston Moor in 1644.

Opposite top. Not much survives of the original Wentworth Woodhouse built by Thomas Wentworth, Earl of Strafford and King Charles I's right-hand man who was executed in 1641. Today's building is the merging of two 18th century houses, erected for the same man, into the longest fronted English country house – all of 600 feet.

Opposite bottom. There are two halls at Burton Agnes midway between Great Driffield and Bridlington. One is a Norman manor house (1170s). The other pictured here was built between 1601–10 for Sir Henry Griffith, a member of the Council of the North, based in York, which was abolished by the Long Parliament in 1641.

Below and right. Dominating Wensleydale, Bolton Castle is one of the most important examples of 14th century secular architecture because of its five star status. It is more comfortable and elegant than earlier castles, even though it is well fortified. The best state suite was allocated to Mary Queen of Scots during her imprisonment there in 1568. It has just celebrated its 600th anniversary and because of its magnificence has latterly become a film set for *Elizabeth* and *Ivanhoe* and for Yorkshire's more modern TV blockbuster series, *All Creatures Great and Small* and *Heartbeat*.

If you want to see how the English castle evolved from defensive earthworks to defiant buildings, go to Helmsley. Walter Espec, a courtier, lawyer and soldier, threw up these large earthworks in the 1120s. Then Robert de Roos I added a wall with towers as further defence of the closed area. In the mid-13th century Robert de Roos III built barbicans to the north and south. King John found it impregnable when he was trying to show Yorkshire's cussed barons who was boss. And, Parliament selected it as one of eight Yorkshire castles to be rendered incapable of use in war. Now the castle walls are decorated with the beautiful, pink, fairy foxglove in spring.

The headland on which Scarborough Castle stands was one of five Roman coastal look-out stations in Yorkshire to give early warning of invaders from the North Sea. There is evidence of its defence associations right back to the 6th century BC. And these associations continued right up to the First World War when the castle was damaged by German shelling in 1914. A lawless baron, William le Gros built an unauthorised castle there around 1138. It was taken over by Henry II who erected a tower keep and retained it as a royal castle. It was besieged by Parliamentarians in 1645 and 1648, became a barracks during the Jacobite rebellion and was garrisoned during the Napoleonic Wars.

The Power and the Glory

St Hilda was a remarkable woman quite apart from her saintliness. She was the second abbess of the 7th century monastery at Hartlepool before she crossed the Tees and made her way down the Yorkshire coast in 657 to found Whitby Abbey for monks and nuns. Its remains stand witness to nearly 1,400 years of Yorkshire's faith.

St Hilda was remarkable not least for the reputation which her religious community quickly established for both justice and devotion. Within seven years it brought the differing Christian missionaries in the North of England together in a synod to chart the way forward. Among those attending was the young St Wilfrid who laid the foundations for Ripon Cathedral. Whitby must have been an exhilarating place for one of its monks was Caedmon, the herdsman who became the first Old English Christian poet.

Sadly, St Hilda was ill-rewarded in death. Both Hartlepool and Whitby were destroyed by the Danes in the 9th century. Whitby was refounded after a visit in the 1070s by Reinfrid, one of William the Conqueror's knights, as a Benedictine house. The designers under-estimated the regard in which St Hilda was held. They simply could not cope with the pilgrims she attracted and a major rebuilding began in the 12th century. Today's ruins are a dramatic memorial to her.

Yorkshire's incomparable Christian heritage began in the 7th century. Two places laid the foundations: York and Whitby. It was in York where it began with the conversion of Edwin, King of all he surveyed across Yorkshire's broad acres, and where he built a tiny wooden forerunner of York Minster for the occasion. It was in St Hilda's Abbey in Whitby 33 years later that the Synod of Whitby marked a vital turning point in the development of the Church in England. There the early missionaries decided to follow the Roman rather than Celtic usages.

The Danes made a terrible mess of the physical expressions of faith in Yorkshire. They sacked York and razed Whitby to the ground. Only some carved stones remain of the Anglo-Saxon monastery founded at Lastingham, on the southern edge of the North York Moors, by Ethelwald, one of four brothers, all priests, three of whom became bishops and two of them saints – Cedd and Chad. The Normans revived the faith and York Minster, Whitby Abbey – or its cliff top ruins – and St Mary's Church, Lastingham all date from the late 11th century.

By the time of the Reformation there were about 70 religious houses – abbeys, priories, friaries and nunneries – stemming from the Conquest and religious orders on the Continent. These fugitives often came in protest against the wealth and corruption they left behind. The Benedictines and their offshoot, the Cluniacs, and the Augustinians, the Black Canons, all settled in Yorkshire. But it was the puritanical and industrious Cistercians, another Benedictine breakaway, who left the loveliest, the most inspiring and most moving mark on the Yorkshire landscape. Witness Rievaulx, Fountains, Jervaulx and Kirkstall, to name only a few of their 20 houses in Yorkshire. Nowhere else in England are such glorious Cistercian remains to be found.

York Minster, England's largest cathedral by volume, bridges the gap from Roman Catholic to Anglican/Protestant England. It stands in all its imposing witness at the heart of a city which for a long time was the country's second ecclesiastical and administrative centre. York itself is a celebration in stone of virtually 2,000 years of Yorkshire history. Ecclesiastically, not much happened after the Reformation for another couple of centuries until Yorkshire was stirred by the fire and brimstone of the Nonconformists. Theirs is part of another story of Yorkshire, cradle of the Industrial Revolution.

The local townsfolk of Selby saved the magnificent abbey church (right) for parochial use.

It was founded by a monk from Auxerre who brought with him the dried finger of St Germain. The main building began around 1100. Its troubles started in 1690 when the central tower fell, severely damaging the south transept. Restoration in the 19th century was swept by fire in 1906. The main repairs took six years to complete. Happily a 15th century font cover was rescued from the fire and much 15th century glass was restored to the east window. Some unique stone figures (below) look down on worshippers.

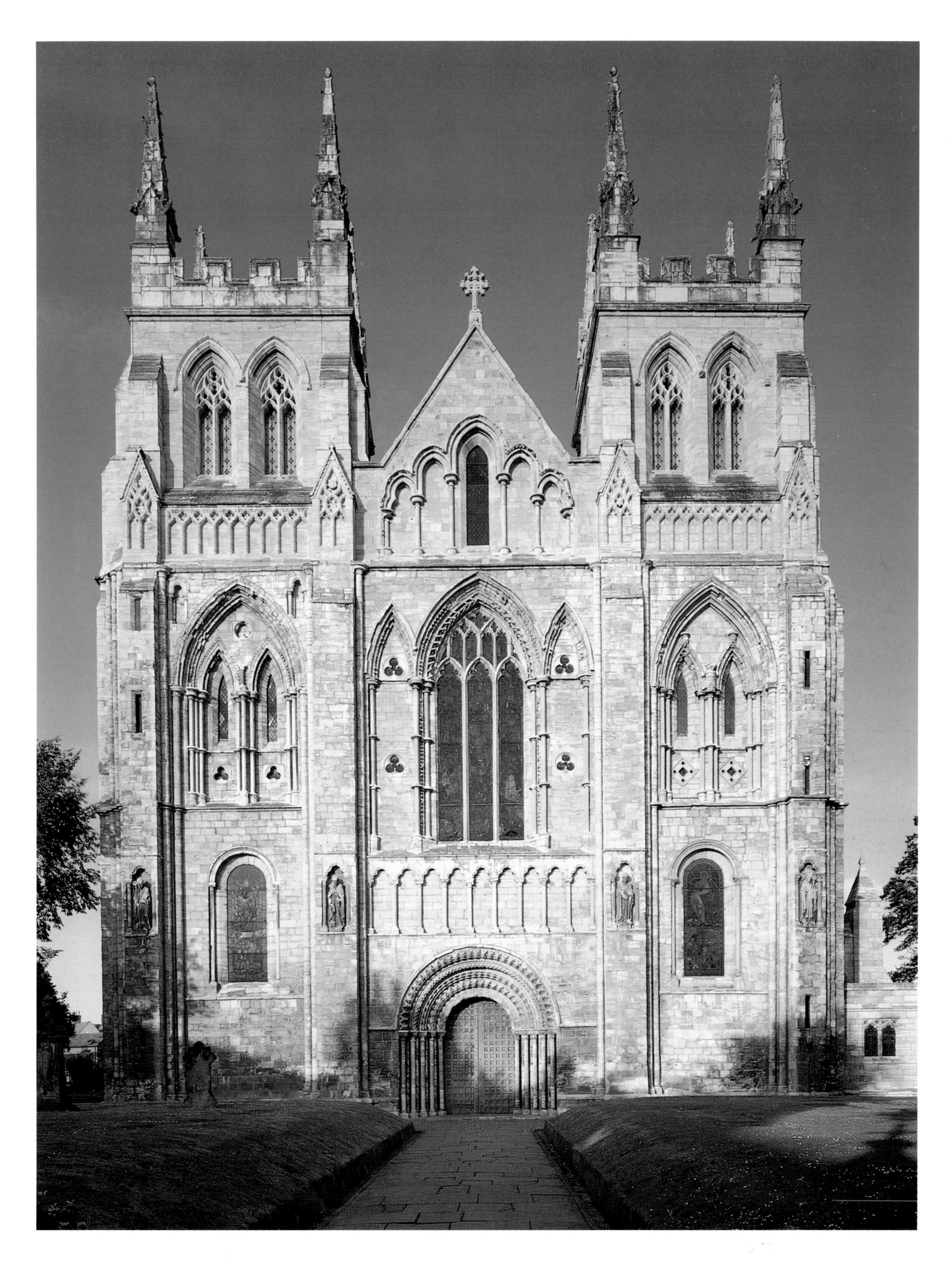

Here on the Plain of Holderness, once submerged under the North Sea, has risen a parish church of breathtaking beauty. It is St Patrick's of, inevitably, Patrington. It is one of the wonders of Yorkshire's ecclesiastical architecture because it is a glorious example of the English Decorated period. It was built like a cathedral on a grand scale in a continuous construction programme over 110 years from about 1310. Its spire soars 198ft above the rich farmlands.

Inside St Patrick's you might imagine it was dedicated to the carver's art. Among its glories are about 200 carved stone faces – human, animal and grotesque – looking down on the congregation from columns, arches and roof.

The arms of Walter Skirlaw, Bishop of Durham from 1388–1405, are to be found in a niche in the battlemented parapet of the porch of the Bishop's Palace next to Howden Minster (left). The reason is very simple. This collegiate church belonged to the Bishop and Cathedral of Durham who rebuilt it in the 14th century in this absolute gem of a market town, constructed predominantly in brick with narrow streets of mainly Georgian buildings. Wakefield Cathedral (right) has the distinction of possessing the tallest spire in Yorkshire, all of 247 feet. The church originated in the 12th century but took its present form in the 15th. It was raised to cathedral status in 1888 but serves as the parish church of the administrative centre of the old West Riding.

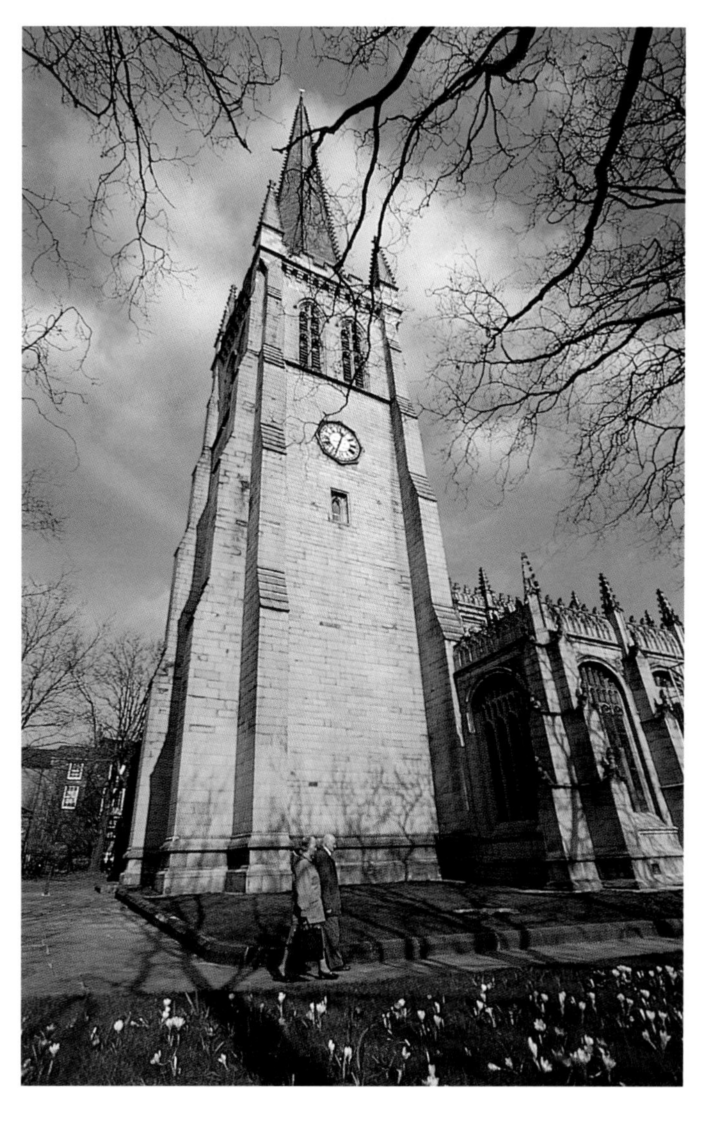

Below and right. Cistercian monks came to Jervaulx between Masham and East Witton in the 1140s to breed horses – it is still racehorse country – and are reputed to have discovered the recipe for Wensleydale cheese.

The remains of their handiwork, in honey-coloured sandstone, is one of the top seven Cistercian houses of Yorkshire and is now in private hands.

The estate, set in parkland, is important to our botanical as well as our monastic heritage.

Pages 55-58. The largest Gothic cathedral north of the Alps has grown at the heart of York over 1400 years. The awe inspiring Minster, as you see it today, is probably the fifth building on the site which was first occupied by a Roman legionary's HQ. Bede recorded the first minster as newly built in 627, no doubt for the conversion of Edwin, Yorkshire's ruler. Two Norman cathedrals followed and the present building was complete, after 250 years' work, by the end of the 15th century.

The Minster has survived at least four fires since 1137, the last as recently as 1984 when lightning wrecked the south transept roof. In spite of all these blazes its ancient stained glass windows miraculously survive – in the north transept lancets, known as the Five Sisters, from the 13th century and in the great east window (page 55), larger than a tennis court, from 1405–8.

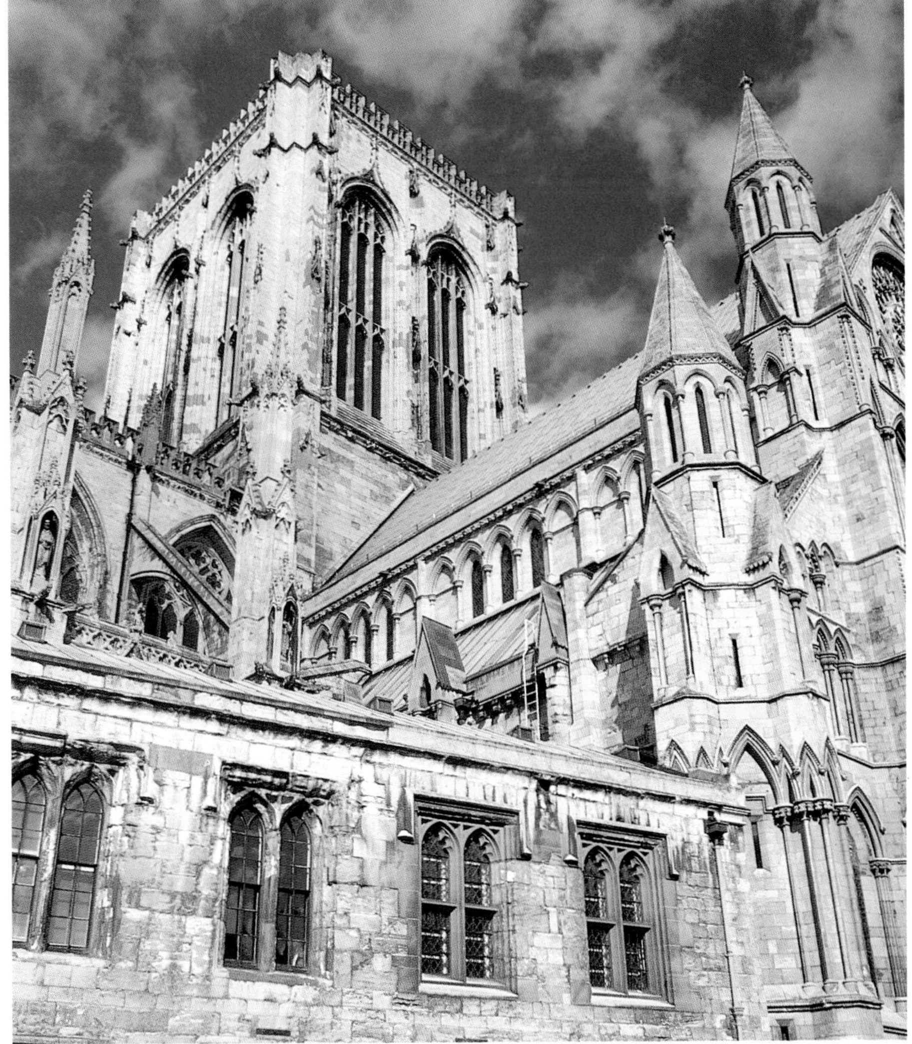

Galtres Lodge
HOTEL
RESTAURANT
YORK COLLEGE FOR GIRLS
David Jason Collection

Right. According to an eye witness Roche Abbey, in the southern extreme of the county, was ransacked by the locals on dissolution. They left such spectacular ruins of the 12th century Cistercian abbey, below the limestone cliff quarried to build it, that Capability Brown incorporated the abbey into his landscaping of nearby Sandbeck Park.

Below. John Wesley, entranced by the beauty of Calder Vale, paid sixteen visits to Heptonstall, a hilltop settlement above Hebden Bridge. He laid the foundation stone for this hexagonal chapel in 1764 believing its design provided better acoustics for preaching. It is one of the oldest Methodist churches in the world.

Leeds' industrial history owes much to Kirkstall Abbey, one of the seven major Cistercian sites in Yorkshire, founded in the 12th century. The industrious, plain-living monks came from Fountains Abbey to work the land beside the River Aire and founded the famous forge. The medieval wool town grew up three miles away and the city has now spread out, around and beyond the abbey. Indeed, the city owns the magnificent ruins which have inspired many artists. They were presented to the municipality in 1889 by Kirkstall's owner Colonel John North, a local millionaire who prospered from bird droppings, nitrate and gas works.

England's best preserved Carthusian monastery, Mount Grace Priory, lies beside the A19 at Osmotherley, against the background of a wooded hillside. It dates back to 1398. English Heritage and the National Trust have combined to give us a splendid representation of medieval monasticism. They bring out the solitary, but otherwise comfortable, Carthusian existence – living room, study with a desk for copying manuscripts, bedroom with its straw pallet and a room for industrial use, with a loom and spinning wheel. One hesitates to mention this, but plumbers will find the ruins fascinating because the gravitational drainage is exceptionally well preserved.

Left. Archaeologists have demonstrated that the nuns of Whitby were industrious as well as pious and an example to the North. In the 1920s they found considerable evidence of their Anglo-Saxon spinning and weaving on the abbey site.

Right. During the 8th century, stone crosses to mark preaching places spread from Durham to Yorkshire and one was planted at Easby, near Richmond. The Church of St Agatha, around which the Premonstratensian canons founded Easby Abbey in 1155, contains a plaster cast of it. Not much is left of the original abbey on this ancient Christian site.

Below. Byland Abbey – see page 65.

The Order of Savigny, from Furness Abbey, took a long time to sort themselves out before redeeming themselves by building Byland Abbey in a wonderful cream ashlar sandstone near Coxwold. Indeed, you could say that Byland is the abbey of false starts.

They were offered a site at Hood, near Thirsk, around 1138 by the Mowbray family but decided it was too small. They upped sticks for Old Byland where they stayed for four years until they could stand its proximity to Rievaulx no longer. The sound of its bells interfered with theirs and since Rievaulx was there first, as Yorkshire's first Cistercian abbey, they felt impelled to move on. At their next resting place – Stocking, near Coxwold – their Order was incorporated into the Cistercians. Abbot Gerold, who had led them on their 40-year peregrinations over a small part of the North Riding, was succeeded by Abbot Roger with whom the monks made their final move to the present site in 1177. They were as unusually generous for the times as they were indecisive for they relocated and rehoused the villagers whose land they occupied.

Once they got down to the work of building an abbey, they erected the largest church in England to a single design, one of the largest rose windows in the country in the west front, half of its circumference being still preserved, and the largest cloisters in a Yorkshire abbey. It is famed for its green and yellow medieval floor tiles (left).

The monks seemed to lead a remarkably peaceful and uneventful existence. History records the even tenor of their ways being seriously disturbed only once. That was in October 1322 when Robert the Bruce, pillaging the Yorkshire countryside, very nearly caught Edward II dining at Byland. The abbey was looted along with Rievaulx.

St Wilfrid became abbot of a monastery at Ripon soon after it was established in 672. He built a particularly fine Saxon crypt, one of only six remaining in England. It was designed to facilitate the flow of pilgrims visiting relics. The church was destroyed by fire in 950 and it was not until the late 12th century that rebuilding of a collegiate church began under the Archbishop of York, Roger de Pont L'Evêque. The magnificent west front dates back to 1220. The seven light east window came 80 years later.

The choir stalls in the cathedral date from the 15th century. They are testimony, with their misericords and canopies, to the skills of the Bromflet family of Ripon wood carvers.

Ripon eventually became a cathedral in 1836. St Wilfrid (right) is still remembered with a carnival on the first Saturday in August in the city which has been a borough since 886.

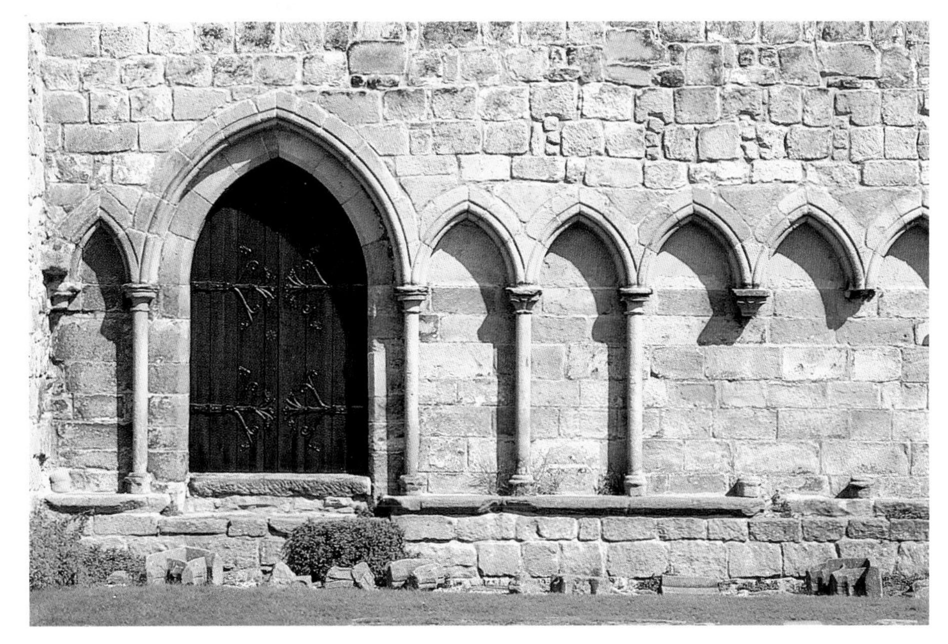

Bolton Abbey – or Priory as it is formally known – is the jewel of Wharfedale. The Augustinian canons were given the land on a bend in the river in 1154 by Alice de Romilly of Embsay, near Skipton, where they settled in 1120. The setting for the multi-coloured sandstone priory has bewitched generations of Yorkshire folk. One of the priory's many restorations in 1728 was supervised by the 3rd Earl of Burlington whose daughter married the 4th Duke of Devonshire. It is to the Yorkshire estate of the present Duke and Duchess of Devonshire that Yorkshire folk now flock.

Left and right. The Early English style is to be found in scores of Yorkshire churches but never to better advantage than in Beverley. The whole eastern half is Early English and the building overall is widely considered to be the loveliest church in Yorkshire, which is saying something. The present building dates from 1220, though the original goes back to around 700. As befits one of England's most prosperous medieval towns, it has in the Minster one of the biggest parish churches in England. Its medieval fittings are of very high quality and it has the finest collection of misericord seats in Britain. In the roof space is a rare 18th century man-powered treadwheel crane to raise building materials to the roof.

Left. J. B. Priestley, Bradford's celebrated writer, loved Hubberholme in Langstrothdale, Upper Wharfedale. Its St Michael's Church has a Norman tower, nave and aisles. But its real treasure – only one of two in Yorkshire – is its rood loft, dating from 1558. This is an elaborately carved wooden balcony to support the rood or crucifix. Most of these were ripped out during the Reformation to eradicate all traces of popery. Pews and stalls were carved by Robert Thompson, of Kilburn, whose trademark – a carved mouse – identifies his handiwork.

Below. Founded by Augustinians in 1120, Kirkham Priory lies in a lovely, wooded valley of the Derwent near Malton. Its founders seemed to be keen on personal hygiene because those in the know say its two-bay lavatorium in a corner of the cloister is "sumptuous". Visitors pass through a late 13th century gatehouse. The ruins of the 12th century nave and west towers are thought to be much as they were built. Members of the de Roos family, Lords of Helmsley Castle, patrons of the priory, are buried here.

Just off the Helmsley to Pickering road is a church dedicated to the Pope who in 597 sent St Augustine to convert the Anglo-Saxons. St Gregory's Minster has an 11th century nave, a 13th century north aisle and a relatively modern west tower, chancel and porch. The porch protects an astonishing sundial over the door. Its Old English inscription describes how Orm rebuilt a ruined church there in the time of King Edward and Earl Tostig, giving the names of the builder (Hawarth) and priest (Brand). This dates the nave at 1055–65 and records the earliest named Yorkshire parish priest. Inside you can find 8–9th century grave slabs, Anglo-Scandinavian cross shafts and medieval tombstones.

What can you say about Fountains Abbey and the Studley Royal estate, near Ripon? It is magnificent and, in spite of its popularity with visitors, wonderfully peaceful. No doubt the founding thirteen Benedictine monks thought so in 1132. To test their zeal for reform, the Archbishop of York gave them a place by the River Skell "remote from all the world, uninhabited, set with thorns ... fit more ... for the dens of wild beasts than for the uses of mankind".

The monks made Fountains England's richest Cistercian abbey. It is now the most complete of its time in Britain and has been designated a World Heritage site. It was incorporated into Studley Royal in 1768 and the whole estate takes in a Jacobean manor, a Georgian water garden and the breathtaking church of St Mary in a deer park with a vista of Ripon Cathedral. Oh the magnificence of it all.

Below. Fountains wasn't very magnificent in the early days. The founders lived in great poverty for two years. Richard, their prior, then went to Clervaux in France to apply to the mother Cistercian foundation to be accepted into the Order. This was granted and on his return a dean and two canons from York, all rich men, joined them. Work began under a master mason, Geoffrey, in 1134. It was almost completed in 1147 when it was destroyed by fire and they had to begin all over again. The cellarium (below), nave, aisles and south transept left standing, date from this period.

Top left, below and right. It is at Rievaulx Abbey, near Helmsley, that it all started. This is the very first of Yorkshire's unrivalled collection of Cistercian abbeys, founded in 1131 by monks from Clervaux in France. It was the mission centre for the north and grew rapidly. Building it presented a problem because Ryedale there is so narrow that the standard monastic east–west plan had to be rotated south of east to fit. There was a lot of rebuilding a century later in the Early English style reflected in the almost complete refectory on the south side of the main cloister.

Another 100 years on, Robert the Bruce looted Rievaulx as well as Byland. On Dissolution, lead from the roof was buried and was not found for another 400 years. Some of it was then used to repair York Minster's Five Sisters window. Rievaulx Terrace, a National Trust property, two miles away, is part of the Duncombe Park estate's landscape – a half-mile grass walk with a Doric temple at one end and an Ionic one at the other. The abbey's memory was perpetuated in the title taken by Harold Wilson, the Huddersfield-born Prime Minister of the 1960s and 70s – Baron Wilson of Rievaulx.

The Venerable Bede recorded the foundation of the 7th century Northumbrian Monastery at Lastingham. St Chad, a pupil of St Aidan of Lindisfarne, sent his brother, St Cedd, to become Abbot. Only carved stones remain of one of the earliest sacred places of England. On its site, destroyed by the Danes, is St Mary's Church, substantially that of the monastery rebuilt in 1078 by Stephen, Abbot of Whitby. Only eight years later the monks forsook their hollow in the North Yorkshire Moors for York. The church has a remarkable crypt dating from its 11th century rebuilding, containing many Anglo-Saxon fragments.

The Augustinian Priory at Guisborough in Cleveland is one of those which fuelled discontent with Henry VIII's Dissolution of the Monasteries. It took a lead in educating young Yorkshiremen and by involving itself in the life of the community had built up a fund of good will among the populace. A rising, "The Pilgrimage of Grace", came in 1536 with, eventually, most of the Yorkshire gentry behind it. It was bloodily put down and the ex-prior of Guisborough was hanged along with many others. Guisborough, founded by Robert de Brus, stands as a tragic reminder that much good was swept away with the bad in 16th century England.

Made in Yorkshire

Yorkshire millowners had a romantic side to them, especially those who took their industry to Holbeck in Leeds. They often paid due homage to their steam engines, housing them ornately while their workers applied spit, polish and oil until they purred. It is a moot point how many of them went on the Grand Tour – they could have afforded it if they could have spared the time off from making brass – but they took a shine to Italian architecture, not to mention Egyptian and Moroccan styles.

You get two for the price of one, as it were, at the "Venetian" Tower Works on Globe Road. Built in 1864 to manufacture textile machinery, its local architect, Thomas Shaw, based the design of his mill chimney on Lamberti's bell tower, or campanile, in Verona, Italy.

Thirty years later when they needed a dust extraction plant, what did local architect William Bakewell do? Why, he erected a second chimney in the likeness of Giotto's bell tower at Florence Cathedral, complete with flagpole.

Not exactly Venetian, but near enough, some would say, for Yorkshire!

The subjects depicted so far in this book have been decisively shaped by God, the Romans, King Edwin (who took the Christian faith in the 7th century) William the Conqueror, Henry VIII, Cromwell and a handful of rich gentry who erected magnificent country houses in the 18th century's age of elegance. This section is shaped by God's gifts in the form of water, wool, King Cotton at the margin, Old King Coal, man's ingenuity and incredible self-confidence and Nonconformist religion. It takes us to the cradle of the Industrial Revolution.

For centuries wool was the basis of much of Yorkshire's prosperity, rooted in farm, domestic spinning and handloom weaving and the pack horse. Water power brought a further stage in industrialisation. But it was the combination of coal, deposited commercially over much of the West Riding south of Leeds, and the steam engine which created one of the great English industrial conurbations east of the Pennine wall and bounded by Leeds, Sheffield and Doncaster.Turnpikes, canals and railways opened up West Yorkshire to itself and the sea (the Irish Sea as well as the North Sea through Goole and Hull).

All this also brought misery. The tensions arising from rapid industrialisation and urbanisation produced Luddism – the pathetic attempt by workers to smash machines to save their handtrade – appalling living and working conditions, militant trade unionism and in Bradford, after a strike at Lister's Mill, the Independent Labour Party. Fortunately, John Wesley also arrived in the 18th century to create a God-fearing, chapel-going, choral community, inoculated by faith, discipline and a sense of belonging against Marxist revolution.

At the same time, Yorkshire was populated with reformers – such as Birkbeck, Oastler and Rowntree and enlightened employers such as Sir Titus Salt. It was also full of self-made men with brass who expressed themselves, secularly, ecclesiastically and civically, in classical style in stone. After the castle, the abbeys and the great country houses came factories, churches, chapels, yes, cemeteries, and not least, town halls in a glorious exhibition of self-confidence, romanticism and one-upmanship. Italy, Morocco and Egypt often inspired the results.

Now in a post-industrial age we are seeing the greening of industrial Yorkshire. New landscapes are being carved out of spoil and slag heaps. And was Jerusalem builded here? We shall see.

Only London has had a Lord Mayor longer than York. The title dates from 1389. The Mansion House is his residence during his term of office. He works in the Guildhall next door where the city's business has been conducted since 1810. The Guildhall was first mentioned in 1256 but was rebuilt and enlarged in the 15th century. In Committee Room No 1 the Scots had their palms crossed with silver by Parliamentarians for handing over Charles I. Being Scots in tight-fisted Yorkshire, they counted out the cash on the table. Under the Guildhall a passageway runs down to a quay on the Ouse where one Lord Mayor kept a skiff for a regular rowing workout.

"Victorian mill owner" conjures up a picture of some miserly, hard Gradgrind taskmaster exploiting his downtrodden workers. There are other sides to the story and the Egyptian mill, deep in the industrial Holbeck area of Leeds, is one of them. It is not exactly how you might imagine one of Blake's "dark, satanic" variety. It was built by John Marshall when he took over his father's linen manufacturing business. Temple Mill, as it is known, was designed by Joseph Bonomi who had clearly been smitten by Egyptian architecture and decoration and adorned the building with ancient Egyptian columns and motifs.

Below. Arguably Europe's outstanding remains of the Industrial Revolution, Lister's Mill – or Manningham Mills, as they are known – dominates part of Bradford, once the world's premier wool centre. Their scale and design reflect the tremendous confidence and power of Yorkshire's entrepreneurs amid much hardship. But they also go down in history for their contribution to Britain's political development and the eventual emergence of the Labour Party. After an 1890–91 strike there ended in the imposition of wage cuts, many trade unionists forsook the Liberals and formed the Independent Labour Party, a forerunner of the party presently governing Britain. It held its first meeting in Bradford in 1893.

Right. Saltaire, near Shipley, gets its name from Sir Titus Salt and the river which flows through it. It is a monument to his commercial success and social responsibility. It all began in 1850 when Sir Titus, who had made his fortune out of alpaca and mohair, decided to leave "the stench and vice of the industrial city" (Bradford) for the clean countryside up the valley and build not only a new mill but a model village for his workers.

Halifax's most noteworthy architectural monument – to the handloom weaver – is its Piece Hall, the only cloth hall left in Yorkshire. It was saved from the demolition men, they tell you, by a single council vote. Thank God for that. The town's cloth merchants banded together to erect a building, opened in 1779, to market their goods by the piece, a measure – hence the name. They built an Italian piazza! – a sloping rectangle enclosed by two or three storeys of colonnaded galleries housing 315 small trading rooms. Renovated in the 1970s, these rooms are now arty crafty shops and the rectangle is used for a market and concerts.

Sir Titus Salt opened his new Italianate mill, then the largest textile factory in Europe, to tremendous rejoicing. Over the next 20 years 820 workers' houses were provided in what is described as mildly classical style on the grid system. Their different sizes were to accommodate not the employee's family needs but his status.

Sir Titus also threw in, if that is the right term, a hospital, alms houses, school, institute-cum-library, a park and church (right), which Nikolaus Pevsner described as the "only aesthetically successful building" there. Its front portico of Corinthian columns curves to form the base of an ornate cupola. The Salt Mausoleum is pictured on the left of the church.

Since the mills closed in the 1980s, they have been put to many new uses including an art gallery housing the world's largest collection of the works of David Hockney, the Bradford-born artist. Saltaire has been reborn. One likes to think Sir Titus would be pleased.

Legend has it that Todmorden is half in Yorkshire and half in Lancashire because the River Calder flows under its magnificent Town Hall. It isn't true. Todmorden is all Yorkshire. But the river's banks were a problem in building the Town Hall (below). A company of businessmen got to ground floor level when they found they didn't have proper title to the land. Eventually, the leading millowners, the Fieldens, remedied that and spared no expense – £54,000 even in those days – on a town hall designed by John Gibson, a student of Sir Charles Barry. It is distinguished for the quality of its stone and internal and external decoration.

In case you think the Sykes of Sledmere were all follies and frivolities, there are other sides to them, including caring. Take, for example, their Wagoners's Memorial (below). It commemorates the Wagoners's Special Reserve of Yorkshire Wolds drivers who provided transport for the Expeditionary Force to France in World War I.

Left. Nestling deep in the Pennines, Todmorden is amazing. This small cotton town of 13,500 souls has produced two Nobel Prizewinners – Sir John Cockcroft, who split the atom, and Sir Geoffrey Wilkinson, the organometallic chemist.

Below. Until the Industrial Revolution, there wasn't much more to Hebden Bridge than the existing distinctive 16th century stone bridge for the packhorse trail. Then the Calder became "the hardest worked river in all England" powering textile mills by the score. It boomed and bust in little more than 100 years. But the town picked itself up in the 1970s and now its warm millstone grit terraces, built on top of each other into the precipitous hillsides, make it a spectacular post-industrial Pennine centre.

It was here that the author was brought up and where he started his journalistic career on the *Hebden Bridge Times*.

Stone Age man hunted here. It is now potholers' and serious walkers' country, the land of the Three Peaks – Ingleborough, Penyghent and Whernside. Cutting through it – and sometimes riding high above it – is the dramatic Settle to Carlisle Railway line which is worth a trip on any fine day. Who said railway engineers didn't relish a challenge?

From around Selside below Alum Pot, one of the better known potholes, the line climbs 200ft in five miles into increasing wilderness inhabited only by sheep and curlew. And then you come to Ribblehead Station which for some railwaymen would be the equivalent of Stalinist banishment to a power station in Ulan Bator. Not surprisingly it became a weather station in 1938 and stationmasters, who were not unduly taxed by passengers, were trained in wind speed calibration and rainfall measurement. Inevitably, they became dab hands at both.

The best is yet to come. It is Ribblehead Viaduct (below), the line's

trademark, as it were. Its 24 tremendous arches span for a quarter of a mile the bog of Batty Moss, carrying the rails 100ft in the rarefied air above the tundra.

The old nationalised British Rail wanted to close the line and cited the cost of maintaining this great structure in support of its case. Yorkshiremen, backed by others, determined to preserve our railway heritage, showed what a fuss they can make when they feel like it. The viaduct was repaired and trains still charge up and down the fells.

Below. Charity begins at home. It certainly did for Lady Margaret, Countess of Cumberland, and wife of George Clifford, the third Earl and Lord of Skipton Castle. She founded the almshouses 400 years ago at Beamsley, near Bolton Abbey, for widows connected with the castle. They were finished by her daughter, Lady Anne Clifford, who also restored Skipton Castle after its Civil War siege.

Doors lead off the chapel, at the heart of the circular, domed hospital, to the 13 houses. Here the widows lived a simple life free of charge according to the rules laid down by the Countess – you had to be fit enough to look after yourself, attend divine service and not absent yourself for more than 24 hours.

For the last 90 years, under the Charity Commissioners, the now modernised almshouses are for poor women of good character who cannot maintain themselves. But Lady Anne's portrait still hangs, superintending her charity, in the chapel.

Below. Over 120 years, Yorkshire's finest necropolis at Undercliffe received 123,000 bodies. They rest overlooking Bradford's mills in which they mostly worked. Brass bought you in death a flamboyant grave on the central boulevard topped by pinnacles, obelisks, temples or sphinx. The poor were buried on top of each other.

Right. Leeds has commercial traditions going back to the 15th century and a wonderfully planned Victorian heart. Its Corn Exchange, by Brodrick, is a fine, oval, millstone grit edifice, originally only for members, each with their round-arched numbered office. Now it has been imaginatively converted into shops.

otto

The city of York presents an unrivalled standing pageant of history. Part of it is the railway station which leads out onto the city walls. Passengers too numerous to count may well have wondered why on earth on the flat York plain they could not have built a straight station over a straight line for what became a major railway centre. The answer is that they underestimated the traffic.

The original gracious station of 1840 was inside the city walls but it soon became far too congested, especially as trains had to go out the way they came in. So in 1877 the North Eastern Railway built a new station over the existing curving line. The magnificent sweep of the ribs of the cast iron arched roof is one of the more unusual views in a city where you are spoilt for choice.

John Betjeman described Huddersfield's railway station as "the most splendid station facade in England". It shows what can happen when Yorkshire rivals settle their differences and decide to cooperate on an enterprise.

The Lancashire and Yorkshire Railway and the Huddersfield and Manchester Railway and Canal companies were originally in hostile competition. They celebrated their accord by engaging a York architect, J. P. Pritchett, to give their station a 416ft long facade with a splendid eight-columned portico, 68ft high, which would not be out of place in Rome.

It forms the west side of St George's Square which speaks in Victorian stone of the quality and substance in this fine old worsted town.

Leeds Civic Hall, completed in 1933, is the seat of the city's government. It looks across a triangular place to the rear splendour of the tremendously grand Victorian Town Hall with which it is inevitably compared. It perhaps reflects some of the uncertainties of the awful decade into which it was born. But it is nonetheless an ambitious Civic Hall with a four-column portico, two Wrenish towers and a tunnel-vaulted reception hall 90ft long. As a reporter, the author covered council meetings in the chamber and has spoken in its marvellous assembly hall.

"One of the most convincing buildings of its date in the country and of the classical buildings no doubt the most successful" – that was the judgement of Nikolaus Pevsner, a stern architectural critic, on Leeds Town Hall. It proclaims the ambition and confidence of the Victorians in all their pomp and circumstance.

The author preferred it when it was still in its muck, before they washed the soot off it. You now see it as it must have looked when Queen Victoria stood before its huge podium of steps and its enormous Corinthian columns at its opening in 1858. The concert hall is just made for Yorkshire's choirs. In 1936 they dined the Jarrow marchers and their dog in the crypt so well that one of them said that after a meal like that they should be able to walk to Canada.

Left. Dewhurst's great mill at Skipton grew out of the Dales' village where the family, originally trading in wool, got in on King Cotton's ground floor. In its early days it heard the Riot Act read over a Lancastrian mob protesting against power looms. Now it is the home of a greetings card manufacturer.

Below. The canal through Skipton is a branch of the Leeds-Liverpool. The 18th century idea was to link the German Ocean with the Irish Sea. Advocates of the Leeds–Liverpool canal – the western half of the link – claimed it would cut transport costs by a factor of twelve – from 12 to one penny per ton mile. Yorkshire and Lancashire Committees were formed to raise the cash and a new War of the Roses promptly broke out. Yorkshire went on fund-raising strike until Lancashire caught up. They did.

BINGLEY FIVE
RISE LOCKS
Nos 25 TO 29
WATER PRINCE
WATER PRINCE

Left. Digging their way up the Aire Valley from Leeds, the navigators, or navvies, building the Leeds-Liverpool canal, came up against a hill at Bingley. They conquered it with a staircase of five locks, now one of the most photographed sights in West Yorkshire.

The locks were excavated by local labour at a rate of threepence ha'penny per cubic yard (or ton) burning a limestone seam with the coal underneath it and using the slaked lime to build the locks with local stone. In spite of such thrift, James Brindley's £260,000 estimate proved spectacularly wrong. The money ran out with the canal only half built.

None of the promoters lived to see its 127 miles completed in 1816 just in time for the railway age. But they have left us a wonderful recreational facility through stunning country.

Below. Understandably, the villagers of Emley, near Huddersfield, were not keen on a new transmitter mast when in 1969 ice and high winds brought down the original 1,200ft high steel television mast on top of the Pennines. Miraculously, nobody was hurt but the Methodist Church was wrecked. The mast was replaced with the tallest self-supported tower in Britain at 1,080ft tall. The landmark has an enclosed room at 865ft.

Below. Grinding corn by a watermill goes back at least a thousand years at Crakehall, near Northallerton. A mill was recorded in the Domesday Book. In medieval times it was owned by the Nevilles of Middleham. It closed 70 years ago but was restored for use in the 1980s. For hundreds of years they managed very well with two storeys until the function of the jolly miller changed in the 19th century to become a dealer for those who did not grow their own crop. A third floor was added to provide dry storage.

Left. The acceptable face of wind power – Yorkshire's last working windmill at Skidby on the Yorkshire Wolds near Hull. Built in 1821 this seven-storey mill ground corn by wind power until 1954 when it went electric. Commercial production ended in the sixties. Restored in 1974, it now operates as a tourist attraction.

Below. Driving or travelling by train between Doncaster and York you pass through one of the great powerhouses of Britain. On either side you keep catching glimpses of huge coal fired power stations. Drax, Eggborough and Ferrybridge which is very difficult to miss. Ferrybridge dominates the junction of the M62 motorway and the A1 – the Great North Road – north east of Pontefract rather like a towering, steaming giant.

Far left. Kingston upon Hull's importance as a port goes back to the 13th century. It handled much of England's wool trade in the 14th century and 200 years later the timber trade brought further expansion. It was a whaling port before it was a huge fishing port. By 1866 some 300 trawlers were based in Hull or the Humber. Now there are very few. More than half its docks, built between 1778 and 1969, have closed but it remains a major conduit handling about a sixth of the nation's seaborne trade.

Yorkshire's two great estuaries – the Tees and the Humber – are bridged in different ways. In the North, the Tees is crossed by the largest transporter of its kind in the world – pictured left – and the only one in Britain left working. It was built in 1911 by Cleveland Bridge to replace a ferry linking Middlesbrough with Port Clarence on the north bank. It carries a gondola which transports up to ten vehicles and 600 passengers.

In the South, the Humber Bridge – pictured overleaf – makes the Guinness Book of Records with the longest span in the world – all 4,626ft of it – and the siting of the 533ft high towers allows for the curvature of the earth. It will go down in history as a rather expensive by-election promise as the interest on the debt soars. It took nine years to build and cost £96m. The Queen opened the magnificent span in 1981.

When the author first went underground in 1961 as an industrial correspondent – at the Prince of Wales colliery at Pontefract – pithead gear (and spoil heaps) were the commonest sight over a huge chunk of the old West Riding bounded by Leeds, Wakefield, Barnsley, Sheffield and Doncaster. The National Union of Mineworkers sent 106 delegates to its council meeting in Barnsley – and the industry was shrinking even then.

There is little left of the now-privatised coal industry, though curiously the Prince of Wales colliery is still producing. Yorkshire's richest seams lie in the relatively recently developed Selby coalfields to the east. The industry declined precipitously after a year-long strike in 1984–5. Industrial diversification is now the name of the game in the old coalfield and new landscapes are being sculpted out of redundant colliery sites for theme parks, recreation and industry.

The Yorkshire Dales are not just a pretty face. They have seen a lot of lead mining in their time, especially in Swaledale. The heavy ore was refined on site to reduce its weight before being transported. The ghostly remains of their smelting mills can be seen today as, for example, at the Surrender mine in Arkengarthdale which cuts north out of the main dale at Reeth. Other remains in the area can be seen at Marrick and Grinton where the flue runs up the hillside to carry the fumes away. Not far from Surrender is what appears to be a quaint hexagonal chapel in a field. It is, in fact, an 1804 powder house where they kept the explosive for blasting.

Right. One of the best surviving medieval guild houses in Britain lies hidden behind its gatehouse in Fossgate, York. It is the Merchant Adventurers' Hall built for the Guild of Our Lord Jesus and the Blessed Virgin Mary in 1357. The limestone came from Tadcaster, the bricks from Carmelite Friars in York and the oak from trees at Thorpe Underwood near Selby. The guild established a hospital in the Hall in 1372 and was absorbed into the Guild of Mercers and Merchants to become the Company of Merchant Adventurers of the City of York under a charter of 1581.

Opposite. Quality steel and cutlery: these are synonymous with Sheffield which became a mighty forge on the back of its close proximity to iron ore and Yorkshire coal. But its cutlery trade really took off when Harry Brearley developed stainless steel. This eighth child of country folk sucked into Sheffield by the Industrial Revolution, so disliked school that he described his childhood as that of "a Sheffield Street Arab". His fascination was with steel making. His discovery of how to get the right blend and treatment of high chromium steel ended for ever the problem of rusty knives, forks and spoons. It also had manifold applications from aero engines to space exploration.

ROXY
BARCLAYS BANK

THE ROYAL BATHS

The author has spent a lot of time in Harrogate as a reporter covering conferences. He cannot honestly say that what he heard was always as stimulating or intelligent as he imagined it was when this spa was the meeting place for northern society and especially the intelligentsia. Its stone testifies to its substance; the Stray, its vast green open space, to its values; its gardens to its floral taste and its coat of arms (below) to its civic pride. Its Valley Gardens were created to commemorate Queen Victoria's Golden Jubilee. What a tribute!

The Royal Pump Room in Harrogate (left) is at the town's heart. Its imposing stone dates from 1842 to house the Old Sulphur Well and now contains a museum. Its Turkish baths show how the town can indulge the hedonists among us.

Some would say Harrogate is snooty. It demonstrated otherwise as long ago as 1936 when the rich in their Rolls-Royces pressed fivers on the Jarrow hunger marchers through the windows of their posh cars.

Harrogate is a very fine town indeed.

Country Life

They play cricket everywhere in Yorkshire and not always in as idyllic a setting as this in the village of Crakehall, near Northallerton. The author often played on pitches well over the 1,000 feet contour up in the Yorkshire Pennines. Skylarks sang their heads off above him in the outfield just as they were doing on the fringe of the moor across the valley where another match could be seen in progress.

What's more, Yorkshire cricket is highly competitive – and always has been – with its league structure. Now it is fired with the enthusiasm of the immigrant community from the Indian subcontinent. This is the county which has produced an endless procession of giants of the game – Sutcliffe, Holmes, Rhodes, Hirst, Emmott Robinson, Leyland, Verity, Hutton, Trueman and Boycott. We all hope there are giants to come to restore Yorkshire to its pre-eminence in the county championship.

Most of Yorkshire is green, though its moors are regally purpled with heather in August. It is getting greener as the ravages of the Industrial Revolution are repaired. Yet, even at their worst, Yorkshire's cities were easy to escape from into a wonderful, refreshing rural environment. Indeed, Yorkshire's industry often lived – and to some extent still does – cheek by jowl with the working countryside.

Another feature of rural Yorkshire is its variety. All three ridings are breadbaskets and vegetable patches, but in the Pennines, Dales and North York Moors they concentrate on sheep, milk and beef. A rough dividing line is the A1, which the Romans ran along a line of firm, dry, magnesian limestone from Danum (Doncaster) to Cataractonium (Catterick). The Pennine Way, a 270 mile hike from Derbyshire to the Scottish border, climbs 2,273 feet to the summit of Penyghent, one of Yorkshire's Three Peaks. Railway engineers took on the challenge of the Pennines and the North York Moors with spectacular results as the Ribblehead viaduct demonstrates.

The Yorkshire Dales are a joy to behold. Their trademark is that of the drystonewaller who has woven his patterns across Yorkshire's landscape with just as much aesthetic effect as Capability Brown achieved much more expensively for the great landowners to the east. Town meets country at innumerable agricultural shows. The largest, on a permanent site in Harrogate, is the Great Yorkshire which for 132 years has been showing Yorkshire townies just what the countryside can achieve.

Yorkshire's countryside is full of quaint customs. In Scarborough they all go skipping on the foreshore at the sound of a noonday bell on Shrove Tuesday. In Mytholmroyd, Ted Hughes' birthplace near Halifax, they hold the Dock Pudding World Championships, a highly localised spinachy sort of dish which tastes far better than it looks. In Ripon they have been blowing the Wakeman's horn to set the watch at 9pm since 886.

Rural Yorkshire also hides fancies and follies by the score. The Sykes of Sledmere were in the folly building business for 150 years. "There's nowt so queer as fowk", as they say in the Yorkshire countryside.

Below. One of the author's favourite walks is from Hebden Bridge up to Top Withens just over the Pennine watershed looking north into the Yorkshire Dales. The almost demolished moorland farmhouse is claimed to be the inspiration for Emily Brontë's *Wuthering Heights*. It certainly wuthers up there.

Right. Built rock-solid in millstone grit, like so many steep Pennine villages, Haworth is Yorkshire's leading literary shrine. It even has signs in Japanese. The Rev. Patrick Brontë and his incredibly talented daughters, Charlotte, Emily and Anne, had no idea what they were starting in this then fiercely unhealthy community where they died like flies from consumption. Now visitors flock up its stone-flagged streets to visit the Parsonage museum where the Brontës lived, take in the atmosphere and roam the moors of Cathy, Heathcliff, Jane Eyre and Rochester. In the valley below, the Keighley and Worth Valley Railway steams up the line where *The Railway Children* was filmed.

RESTAURANT

Below. Life in Goathland – God's Land – 500ft up in the heather of the North York Moors, has been much disturbed by technology. Not much had happened since 1117 when Whitby Abbey established a hermitage here. Then the railway station came in 1865 and the village expanded along the mile from the station to the few cottages by the church. And then, a century later, came the television programme *Heartbeat*. Things have not been the same since, though the free range sheep still "mow" its grass verges to perfection.

Left. Yes, this is Nora Batty country: the steps, railings and up and under houses of Holmfirth where the TV series *Last of the Summer Wine* is filmed. The best advertisement Yorkshire has ever known – the sun always seems to shine on Compo, Clegg and Truelove.

Below. They administer the North York Moors National Park from Helmsley. But the town, set in the pastoral delights of Upper Ryedale, has nothing of the wildness and rigour of those moors. Instead, it exudes comfort. It is, in fact, a pretty historical place with its ruined 12th century castle (page 46).

Life centres on the market square where all roads from Cleveland, Thirsk and York converge on shops, galleries, a working smithy and restaurants – and a statue to the second Lord Feversham whose descendants live at Duncombe Park. A beck flows down from the hills past the creamy yellow cottages.

William Wordsworth and his sister Dorothy stayed here on his way to Brompton, near Scarborough, to meet his future wife, Mary Hutchinson. There is much argument whether they stayed at the Black Swan, a leading moors hostelry, or the Golden Lion which is now a butcher's shop. At all events, Dorothy's diary records that they were very well treated. Of course they were, Helmsley is very well bred.

Left. The Archbishops of York had a manor here at Bishop Burton on the Yorkshire Wolds and, discerning priests that they were, stayed in it in medieval times. Hence the Bishop. Burton comes from the Old English "burh tun" – a fortified place. Milestones on the way are stepped to help you mount your horse. When you get there you might still be in the age of the horse – a truly lovely village with a pond, willows, swans, old cottages and pre-historic remains nearby.

Below. Askrigg probably took its name from an "ash tree ridge" in Upper Wensleydale – a combination of Old Scandinavian and Old English. This market town became a busy little tourist spot when the TV series *All Creatures Great and Small* chose a house near the church as the exterior for Skeldale House, home of James Herriot's veterinary practice.

Pages 120, 121. Thwaite is Old Scandinavian for clearing or meadow. There are a lot of meadows here at Thwaite's Kisdon Hill in Swaledale enclosed bythe classic Yorkshire Dales landscape of stone walls and barns. Cherry and Richard Kearton, pioneer wildlife photographers, were born here.

Left. Stone age enclosures and a Celtic field system have been found near the ancient village of Arncliffe in Littondale through which the River Skirfare, not the Litton, flows. Largely unspoilt, the village has a lovely green. Its St Oswald's Church contains a list of Dalesmen who fought at Flodden Field (1513).

Below. The greatest compliment you can pay a Muker chap is to call him "a terrible sheep man". This is deepest Swaledale sheep country. They are also cultured folk, with their Victorian Literary Institute and Silver Band.

The pictures on these pages are so evocative of Yorkshire rural life – or, in the case of haymaking, as it used to be. Now farmers have liberated themselves to a degree from Yorkshire's uncertain weather by cutting silage, though they still need some hay which requires continuous sun. Dalesbred sheep (left) originate in the limestone country of Craven and their type was fixed in 1920 by Upper Wharfedale breeders. They produce a high quality wool for carpets and tweeds. The local agricultural society's annual show(right) is seen in full swing at Muker in Swaledale.

Oh, the nostalgia of show days gone by. For the author, as a reporter, they were one long round of marquees picking up the judges' awards, checking the spelling of the exhibitor's name and the often exotic titles given to their animals – why are goat breeders so impossibly imaginative? – and looking for stories in the powder rooms of the pens which give you a whole new slant on the art of the cosmetician. It's still the same old story wherever farmers gather seriously to show off their stock. Everything has to look its best – like these sheep at Masham Fair and these wonderful heavy horses, the white feathers around their hooves all fluffed to perfection, waiting to be judged at Wensleydale Show. If you're a lucky reporter you might take time off to try something fancy yourself such as hitching a lift on the Walkington Victorian hay ride.

In Denby Dale near Huddersfield, they baked a huge pie to celebrate the brief return to sanity of George III in 1788. To mark the bicentenary, they poured 3000 kilos each of beef and potatoes and 700 kilos of onions into an 18ft pie dish – the ninth monster to be baked to mark great events. This is one of Yorkshire's many quaint and curious attachments to the past which include The Pace Egg Play at Easter to celebrate the triumph of good over evil. In Helperby (below) and three miles away in Aldborough (left), they dance a lot – especially on May Day. Aldborough, near Boroughbridge, on the Great North Road, is one of the few places in England with a continuous record of human habitation pre-dating Roman times and built on the site of extensive Roman remains.

The author has been hiking up to Stoodley Pike for 60 years. It's a kind of pilgrimage – homage to his grandfather, Greenwood Horsfall, who first took him there. This 130ft high stone obelisk, blackened by Lancashire cotton soot, standing sentinel between Hebden Bridge and Todmorden 1,310ft up on the western wall of Yorkshire, isn't, as so many believe, a war memorial. It is, in fact, a peace monument. The Quakers, Nonconformists and Dissenters who held sway in these parts were against war. So when Napoleon was exiled to Elba they opened a subscription to celebrate the "peace concluded in the year of Our Lord 1814".

The first Pike looked nothing like the present one. It was described as "summat like a mill chimney 113ft high, tapering to the top with a 150 step staircase inside". Work on it stopped when Napoleon escaped and was not finished until just after Waterloo. In 1854 it fell down just as the Crimean War was about to break out. A bad omen. But within a week they were raising the £812 needed to build the present obelisk with its 360 degree balcony 40ft up in the prevailing south-westerlies.

In the spring of 1965 the author, then on *The Guardian*, covered the opening at Malham Tarn of the Pennine Way, a 268-mile route from Edale in Derbyshire to the Scottish border. Penyghent is the first "mountain" – as Wainwright of the Way insists it is at 2,273ft – going north from Malham. It is a limestone mound with a millstone cap. You can reach it across Fountain's Fell, a tribute to Fountain's Abbey which before the Dissolution owned vast tracts of land in this desolate area. Penyghent forms with Ingleborough (2,373ft) and Whernside (2,414ft) The Three Peaks which dominate Ribblesdale and present a 25-mile challenge to marathon walkers, fell runners and cyclists whose stamina they fully test in the high country of Yorkshire.

Heritage Coast

The Viking leader Thorgils Skardi ordered "Skardiburgh" to be built at the end of the first millennium, but *Homo sapiens* had lived here on Castle Hill, the promontory separating two bays, for centuries before that. Its 12th century castle has a long and bloody history. But then the Victorians came on their new fangled trains and made it England's oldest holiday resort.

Yorkshire's 100-mile coast rises from the sea at Spurn Head's sand bar at the mouth of the Humber to the highest point on the English East Coast, the 666ft high Boulby Cliffs in the north-east corner of the county. It is dotted with holiday resorts of varying fortunes since Britain started colonising the Continent in July and August – Bridlington, Filey, Scarborough, Whitby and that creation of Teesside ironmasters, Saltburn.

Geographically, it is divided by a spectacular four-mile chalky projection of the Yorkshire Wolds into the North Sea at Flamborough. South of Flamborough there are unbroken sands in front of boulder clay cliffs for nearly 40 miles until they run out in the shifting outlines of Spurn Point at the mouth of the Humber. Going north, the coast becomes ever more rugged, sheer cliffs often falling straight into the sea, until it dips down to the South Gare breakwater which guards the mouth of Yorkshire's other great commercial river, the Tees.

To the south, the Plain of Holderness is rich farming country which claims in the parish church of St Patrick in Patrington village the most glorious example of the English Decorated style. It is on an amazing scale and was begun in 1310. Holderness – and with it Yorkshire – has been shrinking since Roman times. The boulder clay coast is meat and drink to the North Sea and over the last 2,000 years a strip of land 35 miles long and up to two miles wide has been lost along with 30 villages.

It is a different, cliffy coast to the north of Flamborough. Roman sentinels kept watch for invaders from Scarborough's Castle Hill promontory, separating the resort's two bays. It is where Captain James Cook served his apprenticeship to the sea and it was from Whitby that he set sail to open up the world. That same place, Whitby, played a crucial role in the development of Christianity in the 7th century and may the stark cliff top ruins of its abbey let us never forget it.

The wild, inhospitable North Yorkshire coast was also a land of whalers, fishermen, smugglers and shippers of minerals mined in the rich hinterland. Robin Hood's Bay, Runswick Bay, Port Mulgrave, Staithes and Marske all had their day. Now it is Redcar's turn, home of the largest integrated steel plant in Europe. Between the Humber and the Tees and bounded to the east by the coast and the west by the Pennines lies the inspiring heritage which Yorkshire passes to a new century and a new millennium. Let's hope they take good care of it.

The North York Moors are – or were – rich in commercial minerals and Port Mulgrave, near Hinderwell, between Runswick Bay and Staithes, was built in 1857 to export one of them – iron ore – to Teesside's blast furnaces. They built cliff top terrace houses for the workers – Long Row and West Row – and bungalows for the managers. All these houses and the offices of the enterprise are occupied but, down below at the foot of the cliffs, time and the sea have ravaged the port since it shipped its last in 1921. But how, you may ask, did they get the 3,000 tons of ore a week from clifftop to barge and paddle steamer? The answer is by trucks through a mile-long tunnel – visible in the picture below – cut back inland from the staithes. Little remains of the piers and the tunnel has been sealed.

Down the lane inland from Port Mulgrave is Hinderwell which has been called many things in its time: Hilderwell, Hylderwell and Hildrewell. It gets its name from St Hilda, founder of Whitby Abbey in the 7th century. The village churchyard is the location of St Hilda's Well, which is said to have been blessed by the abbess while seeking solitude here.

If there is one thing seagoing man has always needed, it is a lighthouse on Flamborough Head just north of the holiday resort of Bridlington. The latest (right) at its extremity shines out its warning 214ft above the sea for Flamborough is where the Yorkshire Wolds project their chalk four miles into the North Sea in a wonderful display of white cliffs, rock formations, caves, arches and columns. The old chalk rubble lighthouse (left) was built by Sir John Clayton in 1674 and superseded by the present one in 1806.

The northern cliffs are an important breeding ground for seabirds. Cutting across the peninsula from north to south is Danes Dyke, a largely man-made ravine isolating the head from the mainland. But flint arrowheads found in it show it was perhaps dug 1,000 years before the Danes came to these parts.

Scarborough, "The Queen of Watering Places", has been attracting visitors to its spa since Mrs Farrow, in 1620, discovered a health-giving spring. Forty years later a Dr Wittie, who clearly had all his commercial wits about him, added seabathing to its beneficial properties. Its Theatre in the Round hosts world premieres of works by the celebrated local playwright Alan Ayckbourn.

For 200 years visitors and townsfolk alike have turned out on a Shrove Tuesday for a spot of skipping on the foreshore (below). The tradition is thought to stem from the fact that Shrove Tuesday was, in days gone by, one of the few public holidays. Another explanation is that it was around this time of year that fishermen threw away old rope when they changed from line fishing to potting.

Scarborough's lighthouse (top right) is also a popular attraction. Still working, it was built around 1800 and survived German naval bombardment during the First World War.

Below. Think of Teesside and you think of ICI – Imperial Chemical Industries, one of Britain's gilt-edged investments. Its vast Wilton complex is a post-World War II development – all part of the country's rebuilding after the war. The Government, in fact, gave special planning approval. They needed jobs in the North East which had been ravaged by pre-war unemployment. The ten square mile site became one of the world's major petro-chemical complexes. It is an illuminating sight at night from the Eston Hills. The site is now shared by several companies such as Du Pont, Union Carbide and Enron.

SALTBURN PIER

They built their cliff tramway to last in Saltburn. It's still going strong after 116 years. It was part of the rapid development of Saltburn as a Victorian watering hole for Teesside toffs.

Until the 1860s Saltburn was a collection of cottages adjoining the Ship Inn. The hamlet had a lively history as the centre of a thriving smuggling industry, now commemorated in a small museum adjoining t'Ship. But then a new Saltburn was conceived by the iron and steel barons who were looking for new ways of making money. Saltburn's wooded valley and eight miles of golden sands proved irresistible to a group of Quaker businessmen who formed the Saltburn Improvement Company and completed their town plan in 1861, the year the railway was extended from Redcar.

The new Zetland Hotel had its own railway platform under a glazed canopy. It was now possible for London society to board the train at King's Cross and alight not just at but virtually in their hotel in Saltburn. The pier, Italian gardens, halfpenny bridge, hotels, guest houses and residences followed as well as the tramway. The bridge has gone and the pier has been shortened by a storm. But the rest has survived Saltburn's decline since the 1950s. So, too, has the water balanced cliff tramway. It still lifts passengers the 120ft from the beach and, apart from the replacement of gas power with electric, it is basically the same as when it started work in 1884.

Redcar owes its development as a steel town to the discovery of iron ore in the nearby Eston Hills of Cleveland in the early 19th century. These rich seams triggered steelmaking on Teesside and the growth of Middlesbrough from a village to a major town, while at the same time killing off smaller ironworks at Grosmont and Rosedale in the North York Moors. The furnaces were originally located up river opposite Stockton. But they gradually moved down river through the ironmasters district of Middlesbrough as waste slag was used to recover the marshy margins of the estuary. Eventually they reached Coatham (now the eastern district of Redcar) where they were first tapped on June 12, 1873.

Almost exactly 100 years later a massive new integrated steelworks was built at Redcar. The coal and ore is brought in by bulk carriers by sea, fed into Europe's largest blast furnace, rolled in the mills at Lackenby and then exported by sea through Teesport. Every necessary movement of raw

materials and product is made within the site by its own railway.

Getting to this point has left vast tracts of land on the southern shore of the Tees awaiting regeneration. Yorkshire's most northerly shore is not short of land for development.

Left and below. There are some great tales told in the old cliff-side fishing village of Runswick Bay which is the home of one of Britain's few independent lifeboats. Locals were convinced of the need for one when the RNLI closed down its station in 1978 so they raised the money to buy and run their own. In 1901 the village women launched the lifeboat themselves to save their men caught in a storm in their cobles. The village fell into the sea in 1682 but a funeral wake returning home detected movement, alerted their neighbours and saved everyone.

Legend has it that Runswick children, brought up on plundering wrecked ships, used to pray "God bless Ma and Pa, and send us a good wreck by morning".

The connection between Robin Hood (whom Yorkshire claims as its very own) and Robin Hood's Bay (below) is elusive. Staithes' link with Captain Cook, the world's greatest explorer, is not. He was apprenticed at sixteen to a Staithes haberdasher but after eighteen months went to sea in a Whitby ship. Staithes (left) was first noted in 1451 and Robin Hood's Bay in 1538. Both have an atmospheric collection of cottages on top of each other, crisscrossed by very narrow snickets or lanes. Both have seen better fishing days but Staithes, once a leading shellfish port, still maintains its 500 years' full time fishery. Robin Hood's Bay's main industry was probably smuggling, with its network of tunnels, secret cupboards and doors to beat the excisemen.

Below. Whitby has the setting Hollywood dreams of for a period piece. “Stoopendous, terrrrrific”, you can hear its producers saying. After all, Bram Stoker set scenes of his novel *Dracula* on the 199 steps leading up through Whitby’s old town to the graveyard beside the ruined abbey. Built on the steep banks of the Esk estuary, it is heaving with history, and lively with it, too. On the East Cliff are the jagged ruins of the abbey, dating from 657. On the opposite cliff top, the statue of Captain Cook surveys the harbour from which he first went professionally to sea. Below him is an arch made out of a whale’s jawbone. Whitby was a great whaling port from 1753 to 1833. Its most famous whaler, William Scoresby, invented the crow’s nest.

Right. Another statue of Captain James Cook stands with his schoolroom (now a museum) in Great Ayton where his father was a farm manager. He was born in 1728 in Marton, now absorbed into Middlesbrough, and apprenticed as a haberdasher in Staithes. But it was in Whitby that he served his final apprenticeship to a shipowner, John Walker. The house in which he lodged in Grape Lane still stands. And it was from Whitby’s Fishburn shipyard that he acquired his three ships – Endeavour, Resolution and Adventure – which carried him on his three voyages which changed the world. Surely, Yorkshire’s greatest son.

At 666ft Boulby Head, just north of Staithes, is the highest sea cliff in eastern England. It was also part of the oldest chemical industry in the country which began along the North Yorkshire coast around 1600. This worked the shale to produce the alum needed to make a chemical used by the dyeing industry to fix colour. The process of producing alum crystals was pretty complex and involved seaweed, wood, coal, vast quantities of alum shale and human urine which, believe it or not, was often imported from more populous parts of the country down south. It all went swimmingly, if that is the right word in the circumstances, until 1855 when Yorkshiremen in Goole came up with an alternative process using coal waste. A year later synthetic dyes which didn't need fixing at all did for both kinds of shale. Boulby struggled on until the early 1880s.

As this book shows, the last 2,000 years have been a tremendous struggle for Yorkshire folk. But it's been worth it. Just look at it now, as you have done in these pages. What a county!

Photographic acknowledgments

Dorothy Burrows : 16, 50 (left), 50 (right), 52 (right), 66 (top), 83, 84 (bottom), 90 (bottom), 106 (top), 106 (bottom), 111.
David Coates : 8.
Richard Cochrane : 21 (top), 30 (middle), 39 (left), 63 (bottom), 74 (top), 75 (top), 103.
Jacqui Cordingley : 30 (top), 30 (bottom), 85 (left).
Chris Craggs : 22 (right), 53 (left), 59 (top), 100 (top), 140.
Alan Curtis : 33 (left), 43 (bottom), 52 (left), 62, 65, 68, 69, 71 (bottom), 85 (right), 104/5, 118 (top), 128, 132, 131 (left), 135 (top).
Deryck Hallam : 9, 23, 26 (bottom), 29, 32, 42, 61, 72 (left), 80, 124 (bottom),139.
Granville Harris : 40/41, 55, 60, 78, 81.
Roger Kilvington : 35, 45, 47, 56.
Mike Kipling : 21 (bottom), 38 (right), 41 (top), 48, 63 (top), 76, 77, 116 (bottom), 119 (bottom), 130, 131 (right), 133 (top), 133 (bottom), 136/7, 142 (top), 143.
John Morrison : 18, 67 (top), 84 (top), 87, 90 (top), 99, 112, 116 (top), 118 (bottom), 119 (top), 123 (top), 138, 141, 142 (bottom).
Tom Parker : 127.
Ken Paver : 6, 70 (top), 71 (top).
Stuart Price : 75 (bottom), 108.
Colin Raw: 13, 31 (top), 36, 57 (top), 57 (bottom), 73 (right), 91, 92, 94, 95, 96, 97, 101, 102 126.
Roger Redfern : 43 (top).
Paul Ridsdale : 2, 22 (left), 26 (top), 31 (bottom), 37 (top), 53 (right), 72/73, 74 (bottom), 110, 122.
Clifford Robinson : 124 (top left), 124 (top right), 125 (top), 125 (bottom).
Tony Rostron : 123 (bottom).
David Tarn : 20, 24/25, 27 (bottom), 33 (right), 34 (top), 34 (bottom), 37 (bottom), 44, 46, 51, 54 (bottom), 67 (bottom), 70 (bottom), 88/89, 107, 117, 120/121, 134.
Simon Warner : 12, 28 (top), 28 (bottom), 39 (right), 54 (top), 58, 59 (bottom), 82, 86, 93, 98, 100 (bottom), 114, 115.
Keith Watson : 27 (top), 38 (left), 64, 66 (bottom), 135 (bottom).

Page 109 photograph supplied courtesy of Destination Sheffield Ltd.